Manager's Guide
to Mentoring

Other titles in the Briefcase Books series include:

To learn more about titles in the Briefcase Books series go to
www.briefcasebooks.com

Manager's Guide to Mentoring

Curtis J. Crawford, Ph.D.

New York Chicago San Francisco Lisbon
London Madrid Mexico City Milan New Delhi
San Juan Seoul Singapore Sydney Toronto

1 2 3 4 5 6 7 8 9 0 DOC/DOC 0 1 0 9

ISBN: 978-0-07-162798-6
MHID: 0-07-162798-7

This is a CWL Publishing Enterprises book developed for McGraw-Hill by CWL Publishing Enterprises, Inc., Madison, Wisconsin, www.cwlpub.com.

McGraw-Hill books are available at special quantity discounts to use as premiums and sales promotions, or for use in corporate training programs. To contact a representative please e-mail us at bulksales@mcgraw-hill.com.

The *Manager's Guide to Mentoring* is dedicated to all managers who demonstrate extreme personal leadership in their pursuit of excellence while inspiring their employees and serving their shareowners. Further, the *Manager's Guide to Mentoring* is dedicated to all mentors and mentees who have the opportunity to pursue their long-term career aspirations by participating in the mentoring game.

Again, as always, Gina, a special thanks!

Contents

Preface

Now is the time for senior managers to demonstrate the type of leadership that will inspire their organizations to seek new solutions to old, persistent problems. Extreme personal leadership (X-leadership as I brand it in my book, *Corporate Rise: The X Principles of Extreme Personal Leadership*) is the foundation for this effort. I define X-Leadership as taking actions to inspire creativity and exceptional performance, being responsible and accountable, and consistently striving to make the impossible possible.

Mentoring should be one of the first tools deployed in developing X-leaders who will ultimately build and maintain long-term shareowner value. Extreme personal leadership may be the last long-term sustainable competitive advantage for managers in corporate America. In our globally competitive environment, leading-edge technology is insufficient, by itself, to raise corporations out of the current economic quagmire. While technology will continue to be essential to improving productivity, it will not save us from our problems. Simply building products that are smaller, cheaper, faster, and more reliable will not resolve any current economic difficulty. Instead, extreme personal leadership is the key to the future. Extreme personal leadership, however, has always existed, and the supply is theoretically unlimited. It is the new frontier, offering unlimited opportunity. Mentoring should be at its core, for comprehensive personal leadership development programs.

There are many factors that influence corporate success. Certainly, technology is one of them. Others include timing and sometimes pure luck. However, most often, personal leadership is the most substantial factor in leading corporations to sustainable levels of excellent performance.

A major touchstone of our work at my leadership development company, XCEO, Inc., is our steadfast belief that impressive and successful companies have talented leaders and managers. We believe a company will never hit its stride with weak managers. Therefore, extreme personal leadership will always be in vogue.

Corporations must find creative ways to invest in their high-aspiration and high-potential employees. They must increase the supply of qualified individuals who are enlightened and willing to assume the increasing risk and responsibilities associated with serving shareholders as dedicated senior executive leaders.

The current environment should remind all managers how important it is for highly enlightened corporations to value employee leadership development as a collaborative responsibility of individual leaders, line managers, and the senior leadership team.

Corporations that maintain a commitment to developing their high-potential and high-aspiration employees are more likely to be better positioned for recovery from the devastating lows of 2008 and 2009. Effective mentoring will be a key factor in accelerating employee growth potential and improving long-term shareowner value.

The Purpose of This Book

Most leaders and professionals who are at the top of their game or in pursuit have either a mentor or a coach. For high-potential individuals who are the best in their field or aspire to be the best in their field, a personal mentor can make a significant difference between playing and winning. To achieve the highest levels of their capability, they will require a mentor and possibly a coach. Very few professionals have ever achieved substantial success without a mentor.

The roots of mentoring can be traced back to ancient Greece and Odysseus, to the relationship between Telemachus and Mentor. Throughout time, mentoring has been a simple process that links a more experienced individual with someone who is less experienced. The intent is for the mentor to share information and to inspire the mentee to achieve his or her aspirations.

The purpose of this book, *Manager's Guide to Mentoring*, is to provide a broad perspective on the game of mentoring. I refer to mentoring as a game simply to link it to the many mentoring successes in the sports business. It is common practice for new members of a sports team (rookies) to be paired with more experienced players (veterans) to show them the way to effectively integrate with the organization. I recognize that the mentoring process in sports is not perfect. However, there are many examples that demonstrate that mentoring can work effectively. Further, examples in professional sports are generally made more public and therefore we have more insight. Mentoring has been widely practiced in business. However, in business the mentoring process is, understandably, more private and therefore we have fewer examples. The record of success of mentoring in business is hotly debated. However, throughout this book you will find references to several mentoring research projects that indicate the direct correlation between highly motivated employees and substantial improvements in organizational performance.

Overview

Throughout my career, I have implemented several mentoring programs. As a result, I have more than two decades of experience mentoring very successful executives. All the organizations I have been fortunate to be a part of have benefited from the success of the individual mentees. As a CEO and chairman of the board of several corporations, I have mentored a significant number of individuals over the many years. In addition, as a professional mentor, I continue that practice at XCEO, Inc.

Managers have an extraordinary opportunity to influence the careers of every person within their organization. By being engaged with each individual, a manager is in a unique position to provide performance assessments and constructive feedback to increase the individual contributions of each employee.

Extraordinary levels of performance are directly linked to the environment that is created by the organization and its leaders. Therefore, it is important that managers understand what will motivate individuals to build a team environment that encourages and inspires high levels of performance.

Managers have a responsibility to create an environment that encourages each individual to perform at the highest levels of his or her capability. Preparation is the key to success. If managers are not prepared, it is likely they will be ineffective in preparing their employees to achieve great results.

There is a direct correlation between knowledge and engagement. When employees are engaged, they feel better about contributing to the success of the organization. Further, if employees are engaged, they are more likely to contribute substantially better results to the organization.

Conversely, when managers fail to provide opportunities for employees to be appropriately engaged in organization business matters, the less commitment and sense of obligation the employees will feel. When employees are less committed and feel no obligation, they tend to contribute substantially less to the success of the organization. Managers should constantly seek opportunities to keep their employees fully engaged in activities that link directly to the success of the organization.

Managers should not wait for employees to seek out mentors within the organization. Instead, managers should aggressively seek out employees with high aspirations who demonstrate a passion for personal leadership and a desire to contribute substantially to the organization. The most effective managers endeavor to identify individuals who are willing to commit to their own personal development.

Mentoring provides an opportunity for managers to ensure a higher level of engagement within their organizations. Through an effective mentoring program, employees can be exposed to individuals who should provide insight and perspective, which should inspire the employees to seek opportunities to be more engaged in the success of the organization.

In short, mentoring is good for the organization and each of its members.

What's in the Book?

In the first chapter, you will be introduced to differences between mentoring and coaching. Generally, managers provide coaching when employees need to improve their job performance, and they provide mentoring to inspire employees to reach their personal goals and aspirations.

The following three chapters cover the basics of mentoring. Chapter 2 compares managing and mentoring, Chapter 3 examines the need for mentoring, and Chapter 4 outlines what is to be expected from a mentor.

Subsequent chapters will introduce you to several mentoring approaches. They will include professional mentoring (Chapter 5), formal corporate mentoring (Chapter 6), informal corporate mentoring (Chapter 7), peer-to-peer mentoring (Chapter 8), and mentoring from friends and family members (Chapter 9). The remaining chapters explore the details of mentoring.

Special Features

The idea behind the books in the Briefcase Books series is to give you practical information written in a friendly, person-to-person style. The chapters deal with tactical issues, and include lots of examples and how-to information. They also feature numerous sidebars designed to give you specific information. Here's a description of the boxes you'll find in this book.

KEY TERM

Every subject has some special jargon, including this one, dealing with innnovation and creativity. These boxes provide definitions of these terms.

SMART

MANAGING

These boxes do just what their name implies: give you tips and tactics for using the ideas in this book to intelligently manage and encourage innovation and creativity on your team.

These boxes give you how-to and insider hints on techniques insiders use to foster and implement creativity and innovation on their teams.

It's always useful to have examples that show how the principles in the book are applied. These boxes provide descriptions of how organizations prosper by fostering successful mentoring programs.

These boxes provide warnings for where things could go wrong when you're planning and implementing mentoring programs or are a mentee.

How can you make sure you won't make a mistake when you're trying to implement the techniques the book describes? You can't, but these boxes will give you practial advice on how to minimize the possibility of an error.

This icon identifies boxes where you'll find specific procedures or techniques you can follow to take advantage of the book's advice.

Acknowledgments

Once again, I extend my thanks to the XCEO, Inc. team: Belen E. Gomez, Michelle Ronco, Mariam J. Ghazvini, Michael A. Dobmeier, Christina M. Pagkalinawan, Sonia Park, and Fred Dalili. Your excellent teamwork and continuous support allowed me to focus my time and attention om completing the Manager's Guide to Mentoring in record time, without compromise on substance or quality. I personally thank each of you for your commitment to our constant pursuit of excellence at XCEO, Inc.

Our team continues to grow because of your passion for excellence. Again, thank you for the extreme personal leadership and extraordinary support that each of you made to this project. I am forever grateful to each of you!

Belen, this time, you deserve special recognition. The Manager's Guide to Mentoring is a direct result of your leadership in research, development, and editing. As the XCEO, Inc, Brand Manager, you were the critical link to our publishing partners at CWL Publishing. You maintained a positive and tenacious attitude throughout the process. I know it was a bit challenging and tense at times, since you had to maintain your focus on your other responsibilities too, Nonetheless, I hope you enjoyed the experience. Thanks for the extreme personal leadership. This project was a success because of you.

John Woods, of CWL Publishing Enterprises, it was interesting working with you on this project. After a late start, I finally got on the right road. Although, at times, it was a bit frustrating, trying to stick to the map, As a result, I may have wandered off the road occasionally.

In the end, it was a fun and exciting journey. Thanks for your patience and steadfast support. I really appreciated your unwavering focus on consistency and clarity. And thanks John, for your guidance and patience. It was a pleasure partnering with you on this project.

Special recognition goes to the editor, Dr. Robert Magnan, also of CWL. Thank you for contributing so much to the quality of this book. Your track record editing other books in the successful Briefcase Books series worked in my favor. Your contributions to my work are very much appreciated.

Manager's Guide
to Mentoring

Mentoring and Coaching

The need for personal leadership in business is at an all-time high. Personal leadership is, in fact, the last frontier for long-term competitive advantage. I continue to believe that extreme personal leadership is the foundation for building excellence. In this regard, enlightened corporations must strive to incorporate people development into their management gene structure. Therefore, people development must evolve as a core competency for all companies that strive to achieve the highest levels of performance and yield the highest returns to their shareowners.

Managers must learn to view talent as a way of building the long-term value of the organization.

They have a responsibility to identify talent within the organization and turn it into a leadership competitive advantage for the company. Managers must commit to investing time and resources in developing leadership during times of prosperity or scarcity.

All personal leadership development programs should be comprehensive. There should be a variety of approaches available to meet the varying needs of the employees within the organization. Managers must identify how each individual is unique and help that individual develop in such a way as to achieve his or her maximum capability while contributing to the success of the organization.

1

Coaching and Mentoring in Personal Development Programs

There are many tools available to help managers develop their high-performance and high-potential employees. They may choose to construct in-house programs to develop the needed skills or they may take advantage of university and industry-related training programs. While there are many options for managers to consider, coaching and mentoring are indispensable and should always be included in personal leadership development programs.

Coaching and mentoring are two powerful means of helping employees develop. While I emphasize the importance of both programs, coaching and mentoring are not the same.

Researchers have described coaching and mentoring as continuous processes. Neither is a one-time event. Mentoring and coaching are intended to develop individual skills, resulting in improved performance and accelerating personal development. Because of the perceived value of mentoring and coaching programs, they have become a part of the workplace, providing organizations with the opportunity to increase job satisfaction, personnel productivity, and employment stability within their organizations. In fact, with the increase of diversity in the workplace and the accelerated changes in the work environment, mentoring and coaching have become essential components for managers and leaders.

Both coaching and mentoring form a relationship that coaches and mentors describe as a "partnership." However, mentoring and coaching are not the same. It is important for managers to understand the differences.

Differences Between Mentoring and Coaching

At a basic level, it seems easy enough to distinguish between coaching and mentoring:

- Coaching aims to improve performance on the job, in a specific area of skills and knowledge.
- Mentoring aims to develop potential, helping an employee move beyond the job, toward career goals.

- Coaching tends to focus more specifically on present job responsibilities.
- Mentoring tends to focus more generally, to prepare for future job responsibilities.
- In coaching, there usually is a specified time frame for working with the employee.
- In mentoring, the relationship is more likely to be for an indefinite time.
- Coaching typically consists of instruction, training, support, and timely feedback.
- Mentoring is based on education, experience, exposure, and inspiration.

One of the more important differences between mentoring and coaching is that the coach helps the employee do his or her job better and the mentor helps the employee make the transition to self-development and the ability to do other jobs, to achieve goals beyond the present job situation. In short, a coach will help you do what you *need* to do, but a mentor will help you do what you *want* to do.

KEY TERMS

Mentoring Helping an individual develop abilities and knowledge and achieve his or her personal career goals.

A mentor is usually a more experienced person who is also a trusted friend, counselor, or teacher. The role of the mentor is to provide the mentee (or protégé) with insight and direction. The mentor should create an exciting and challenging partnership that inspires the protégé to strive for the highest levels of capability.

A mentor is "a more experienced individual willing to share his or her knowledge with someone less experienced in a relationship of mutual trust. ... A mixture of parent and peer, the mentor's primary function is to be a transformational figure in an individual's development" (David Clutterbuck, *Everyone Needs a Mentor*, Hyperion, 1991).

Coaching Helping an individual develop the abilities and knowledge to do his or her job better, to improve the quality and/or quantity of his or her work, which leads to improving business results for the organization.

Coaching is targeted at improving on-the-job performance, which is usually a requirement for career advancement and usually a condition of continued employment. Usually, coaches are very focused on specific needs of the employees or opportunities to improve their performances. (*Executive* coaching is more like mentoring than coaching.)

Sometimes the term *coach* is used to mean *executive coach*, further blurring the basic distinction between coach and mentor. Thus, when coaching is defined as "Partnering with clients in a thought-provoking and creative process that inspires them to maximize their personal and professional potential" (International Coaching Federation, Code of Ethics, *www.coachfederation.org*), we recognize it as *executive* coaching.

There are many books and articles that purport to define the differences between executive coaching and mentoring. Some of the research suggests that the differences are minimal and, as you would expect, other research suggests, rather strongly, that there are substantial differences between executive coaching and mentoring.

Some of these differences are associated with personal behavior. Some experts suggest that an executive coach will value behaviors that are more often associated with mentoring than with coaching. Some claim the mentor brings career and business knowledge, while an executive coach is not burdened by the clutter and therefore will provide a more independent perspective.

Mentoring and coaching programs are designed to enhance the individual skills that result in improved performance and accelerate personal development. Because of the perceived value of mentoring and coaching programs, they have become a part of the everyday workplace. They provide organizations with the opportunity to increase job satisfaction, personnel productivity, and employment stability within their organizations.

Both coaching and mentoring are "relationship-based" and frequently defined by scholars as "intervention" measures. In the counseling profession, the relationship between the coach, or mentor, and the client is often defined as the "therapeutic alliance." Coaches and mentors describe it as a "partnership." Nonetheless, whether it is characterized as an intervention, alliance, or partnership, it is the foundation for achieving a successful conclusion to the effort.

Further, coaching and mentoring differ in several other ways. Historically, one significant difference has been in the level of formality with both approaches. Coaching programs have been more formal than mentoring programs. However, with the advent of professional mentoring and formal corporate mentoring programs, they are now equal to, or more formal than many other types of coaching programs. Other considerations, such as personal style and particular circumstances, are also important.

Coaching Past

In prior years, coaching carried a negative management perception. It implied that an individual might need remedial assistance to achieve the expected level of performance in the current job. It was used to help marginal performers. In addition, coaching was provided to assist persons demonstrating inappropriate personal behavior that was negatively affecting the business performance.

Coaching: Past Attitudes Prevail

Some continue to view coaching as a sign of weakness and risk. Conversely, the more enlightened managers and leaders see coaching quite differently. They view coaching as a potential competitive advantage for their organizations. Today, coaching is viewed as an investment in the company's best people. Those individuals who are fortunate enough to have a personal coach are viewed as highly valued versus those in risk of losing their jobs.

Coaching, like many other intervention programs, is usually a one-on-one experience. Further, coaching tends to focus on a specific area of improvement, and there usually is a designated term to work on the associated issue. For example, a coach might work with a client for six months to improve his or her "team development" skills.

Focus on Individual Needs

One of the more important differences between mentoring and coaching is that the mentor helps the mentee realize his or her career aspirations. The coach helps the employee perform his or her job better.

Clearly, there is substantial overlap between coaching and mentoring. And, in reality, it really does not matter. It is more important to focus on the particular needs of the individual than to struggle to define differences.

Mentoring can be valuable to anyone in the organization, not just the leaders. A mentor is someone who can be trusted, who will listen, and who will provide candid feedback about concerns important to career advancement. All employees should have the opportunity to be guided by a mentor, but having or being a mentor should never be mandatory. A mentoring program should link the interests of the company to the interests of employees.

A mentor need not be a member of the mentee's department or even work within the organization. A mentor need not be a senior leader; he or she could be the mentee's supervisor or even a more experienced peer. The individual seeking a mentor and his or her supervisor should decide together on a person who they believe would be a great mentor.

Coaching programs should be offered as an integral part of managing. Those who participate in the program—coaches, supervisors, and managers—should be well trained and guided by a process that ensures that employees participate actively in development programs. This helps them develop the skills and knowledge to be successful.

Mentoring, in contrast, is something of a privilege. Individuals should earn the opportunity to be mentored by performing well in their current job responsibilities. Candidates for mentoring are ambitious, upwardly mobile, eager to learn, and seeking opportunities to contribute more to the success of their organizations and to advance in their careers.

Finally, it should be noted that coaching and mentoring are different from supervising in that coaches and mentors provide input that supervisors do not or should not. For example, a coach or mentor might discuss topics unrelated to the supervisor's duties or, in some instances, discuss topics that would be inappropriate for a supervisor to broach.

Mentoring

Although the boundaries between executive coaching and mentoring are sometimes blurred, there is a substantial difference between them. Generally, we look for a coach when an individual is looking for opportunities to improve his or her job performance. However, the coach usually is not expected to have comparable career experience and business knowledge to the person being coached. In other words, for example, some believe a person who coaches a sales executive does not need to have substantial sales experience.

The core principle of coaching is a collaborative, egalitarian rather than authoritarian relationship between the coach and the coached. The primary focus is on developing solutions not analyzing problems. The relationship assumes that employees are competent and have a good attitude. The emphasis is on collaboration between the coach and the coached. The coach does not necessarily need specific expertise in a particular area of learning to be effective. The role of the coach is to expedite goal attainment through a systematic step-by-step process and to help the employee sustain his or her new skills. (For more on this, you might want to check out A. Grant, *Towards a Psychology of Coaching*, University of Sydney, 2001, pp. 1–55.)

Those who study the difference between mentoring and coaching suggest that they meet the requirements of two constituencies. They are the mentee (or the person begin coached) and the organization (see P. Hawkins and N. Smith, "Coaching, Mentoring and Organisational Consulting," Open University: Buckingham, 2006). Further, these researchers believe both coaching and mentoring have generally ignored the needs of the organization. They point out that it's equally important to consider both the needs of the organization and the individual in setting up such programs.

The term mentor derives from Homer's *Odyssey*, in which Mentor was the wise and old friend of Odysseus. When Odysseus left to fight in the Trojan War, he entrusted Mentor with the care, guidance, and education of his son, Telemachus. The generic meaning of a mentor, then, is a parental figure who sponsors, guides, and instructs a younger individual.

We can define mentoring as a caring and supportive interpersonal relationship between someone experienced and knowledgeable and someone less experienced and less knowledgeable. In this relationship, the mentee, or protégé, receives career-related and personal benefits. Mentoring facilitates the transfer of knowledge, skills, attitudes, beliefs, and values. The essence of the relationship is that the mentor takes a direct and personal interest in the education, development, and success of the mentee.

A mentor has a responsibility to always maintain unquestionable confidentiality between himself or herself and the mentee. Trust is the foundation for establishing and maintaining any effective working relationship between the mentor and the mentee. On the other hand, an executive coach is most often expected to report to the supervisor of the person being coached regarding the progress that person is making.

Finally, mentors play many roles, very often including coaching function. However, our focus in this book is on the mentor in the role as a *career facilitator*.

Managing and Leading

It's important for managers to understand and value the differences between their management responsibilities and their leadership opportunities. In general, managers are responsible for producing results by directing the work of others. However, when managers become leaders, they inspire employees to perform at levels that go far beyond the results gained from simply directing their work.

SET THE TONE

Leaders have the responsibility to create environments that inspire their people to perform at their highest levels. Research has shown that employees look to examples given by senior leaders as a way of generating their own motivation. The famed W. Edwards Deming distinguished between *leader* and *manager of people*. He said, "Reserve the word *leader* for individuals who are going to change the world, change the organization." Thus, the label of leader would aptly apply to those who transform their organizations through their knowledge, ideas, boldness, actions—and example.

Extreme Personal Leadership

In my book, *Corporate Rise: The X Principles of Extreme Personal Leadership* (XCEO, Inc., 2005), I discuss how great leaders take exceptional actions that inspire creativity and ever-higher levels of performance. The best managers know how to demonstrate personal leadership, which inspires people to perform at the highest levels of their capabilities. Successful managers are responsible and accountable. Great leaders reach for the stars! I call such leadership *extreme personal leadership* and I call such leaders *X-Leaders*.

Leading from the extreme (in the best sense of that idea) is the practice of going far beyond the boundaries of conventional expectations. It is the pursuit of what may not seem possible from an ordinary perspective. It means setting audacious goals and achieving them while playing by the rules. X-leaders want to win with a passion. They have a very positive attitude. They are results-driven and they are uncompromising in their pursuit of excellence.

Leaders: Born or Made?

Many researchers have tried to determine whether the ability to lead is an inborn personal trait or whether it consists of a set of skills that can be learned. Persuasive arguments support both views, and I see some truth in both.

POWER OF A LEADER'S PRESENCE

FOR EXAMPLE

Michael Jordan, a star player for 15 seasons in the National Basketball Association, was a model of personal leadership. He consistently demonstrated his power to influence the outcome of a game by his mere presence. Even if he was not playing, all the players on the court raised their level of play because they had such great respect for his talents. The sheer strength of his presence brought out the best in all of the players around him as they tried to impress him. Similarly, in the corporate world, the mere presence of a leader in a meeting can bring out the best in others.

However, my experience tells me that the ability to lead is a set of knowledge and skills that can be learned. Much of my own success as a leader is the result of what I learned from some of the best and brightest leaders and visionaries in the corporate world, together with what I gleaned from ineffective leaders.

Many ineffective leaders offer evidence that the power to influence change can come in the form of pure authority granted through political patronage or inheritance. However, the ability to cause change also can come in the form of leadership. In other words, even if an individual is not granted direct authority to make change, he or she still can affect change by using leadership skills. In my view, leadership is an opportunity that can be earned.

Clearly, it takes power to become an extreme personal leader. The source of that power is an ability to lead that comes from within, results from knowledge and experiences. Professional mentors recognize the most effective way to develop the power to influence the outcome of a particular situation is through knowledge and skills. However, a person also can develop power through passion. Mentors who care very deeply about something and effectively show their passion can earn the power to make positive changes in many environments.

Mentors help others develop plans and strategies to realize and achieve their long-term career aspirations. A successful mentor will help the protégé earn the power to influence the appropriate outcomes, which are fundamental to accelerated career advancement and personal growth.

Effective mentors must also be effective leaders. When appropriate, they must demonstrate the ability to function concurrently as personal career advisors and corporate change agents.

A Vital and Delicate Balance

In all situations, the mentor should be working on behalf of the protégé. That does not suggest showing disinterest in the organization where the protégé is employed currently. However, it does clearly imply that the protégé is the primary focus for success.

A mentor might ultimately advise a mentee to seek career opportunities beyond his or her current organization that better fit the mentee's career aspirations. In this situation, the mentor should focus on the interests of the protégé. However, even though the primary focus is on the protégé, he or she should not be insensitive to the needs of the organization. That would introduce a serious conflict of interest, unless the organization has encouraged the mentor to work with the mentee to seek opportunities outside the organization.

When mentors are engaged on behalf of their organization, they have a shared obligation to the protégé and the company. They have the same commitment to both parties. There are no situations where the mentor should be working for the corporation and not for the mentee. I do not recognize any situation where the mentor should be working on behalf of the organization without a commensurate level of commitment to the mentee.

A corporation might hire a professional mentor or designate a formal corporate mentor to provide career services to one of its employees. Although the company is paying for the mentoring services, either directly or indirectly, the desired outcome of those services should be equally as desirable for the individual as for the company. On the other hand, if the protégé is paying for mentoring support from a professional mentor, those services need not necessarily provide benefits to the organization. In other words, if the employee pays, the employee will expect benefits, and if the corporation pays, the organization will expect benefits. Regardless who pays for the services, however, the mentee should be the beneficiary. When the protégé wins, then it is likely that the corporation will win as well, and if the mentee loses, most likely the corporation will also lose.

Mentoring Programs

As I will discuss in the following chapters, there is an obvious investment required to develop and maintain an effective mentoring program. Whether informal or formal, there are costs associated with people development. This investment should be made on behalf of the organization and result in benefits for the same. However, in mentoring, the corporation cannot win unless the protégé succeeds.

The success of a mentoring program should be measured by the success of the participants. If the employees in a mentoring program develop in their careers, it should correlate with improved performance of the organization. On the other hand, if the employees in a mentoring program fail to develop, they are less likely to improve their performance and contribute more to the organization. In fact, if the program fails, they are likely to leave the corporation. That is why corporations should strive to support and improve their mentoring programs, in order to receive a better return on their investment.

Mentoring and leadership development are not optional for corporations seeking to improve their performance in a competitive environment. Those corporations that choose not to provide mentoring services for their high-performance and high-potential employees will evolve into a mediocre state of performance. Average performance from leaders with average development will result in below-average performance from average companies and below-average shareholder returns. Quite simply, companies that do provide mentoring and leadership development for their high-performance and high-potential employees will outperform companies that do not.

Employee development is not optional. Losing high-potential employees has a substantial cost. Studies show that it costs much more to hire peo-

CAUTION

CHOOSE WITH CARE

Not all employees are equally qualified to assume greater responsibilities. Some are smarter than others. Some work harder. Some are more motivated. Although managers should treat all employees fairly, they certainly should not treat them all the same. They are not all equally ready, willing, and able to benefit from mentoring.

ple to replace lost employees than to invest in developing employees. Managers should use mentoring programs to develop their employees, even at the risk of losing some of them, rather than fail to invest in their employees and run the risk that the company will fail.

In order for organizational mentoring or coaching to be effective, the participants and the organization must have clearly defined and aligned learning and development objectives. Equally important, the choice of using a mentor or a coach should be determined based on a common set of needs and learning opportunities and assessed to see which one best fits the needs of the individual.

To succeed in the long term through continually improving, most corporations need to continually improve the quality and effectiveness of their leaders. Managers must create environments in which employees achieve goals through a leadership approach that creates the energy to propel organizations to heights far beyond expectations. Successful leaders realize that their effectiveness is highly dependent on the achievements of others, so they surround themselves with the best people available and invest heavily in developing those people.

Senior managers must make leadership development a core competency if they want highly motivated, high-performance employees. They must hold themselves responsible for creating a stimulating environment that influences the kind of day-to-day business decisions that have a profoundly positive impact on employees and customers.

SMART

MANAGING

"TO WANT THE BEST IN THEM"

One of the 10 keys to great leadership, according to Jeff Immelt, General Electric's chairman and CEO, is to "like people." What does that mean? "It is critical to understand people, to always be fair, and to want the best in them. And when it doesn't work, they need to know it's not personal."

This healthy environment nurtures the dynamic employees and teams that get work done.

Coaching and mentoring are both very important in employee development. However, we must keep in mind the differences between them as we discuss mentoring.

Mentors can be of several types—informal corporate mentors, formal corporate mentors, professional mentors, peer-to-peer mentors, and friends and family members as mentors. We will discuss these types in later chapters. First, we will consider the relationship between managing and mentoring, the needs for mentoring, and what is to expect from mentors.

ALIGN PERFORMANCE AND DEVELOPMENT

SMART MANAGING

A personal performance plan and a personal development plan are not the same. They should be clearly distinct.

However, when they are synchronized, that alignment will speed up the employee's career success. Managers should work with each employee to develop a periodic performance plan. It should be specific, measurable, and driven by the needs of the business. This plan may involve coaching. Likewise, managers should work with each employee to develop a personal development plan. This plan may include mentoring. Furthermore, each development plan should be driven by the needs and aspirations of that individual employee.

Manager's Checklist for Chapter 1

☑ Understand the basic differences between coaching and mentoring.

☑ Be a role model: inspire all employees to do their jobs to the best of their abilities—and inspire those with more potential and higher aspirations to go above and beyond.

☑ Praise your employees for their contributions to the company's success.

☑ Treat all employees fairly—and resist the urge to treat them all the same.

☑ Promote coaching and mentoring.

☑ Make sure that each employee has a personal performance plan.

☑ Encourage each employee to develop a personal development plan.

☑ Develop a passion for developing people.

Managing
and Mentoring

A
s discussed in the first chapter, coaches and mentors play different roles in business. While coaching and mentoring functions
overlap at times, they have distinct characteristics that differentiate them. The relationship between managing and mentoring is similar: in business, managing and mentoring responsibilities also overlap
on occasion. But beyond those situations where their functions overlap,
they each have distinct characteristics that differentiate them, too.

The concept of management commonly focuses on how a business is
run. It generally includes functions such as planning, organizing, supervising, and coordinating activities. The outcomes of all of these functions
depend on the effectiveness of the employees responsible for carrying
out these activities. Therefore, it is imperative that organizations that see
the need to achieve great results be willing to invest in the people they
expect to deliver them.

Successful organizations recognize the importance of effective management. They understand and value the need for personal leadership
development. They understand and appreciate the link between the success of individual employees and the success of the organization. Enlightened managers consider mentoring as one of several leadership
development tools. They incorporate some form of mentoring into their
comprehensive people development activities.

KEY TERM

Enlightened management These are individuals and organizations that have seen the light. They clearly understand the inextricable link between the individual success of the people and the success of the organization. Enlightened persons are experienced, or have gained their insights through other forms of intervention. Enlightened managers recognize that personal leadership is a renewable resource, which is basically untapped. They have the wisdom, or the ability, to understand with great clarity, the value embedded in people. Furthermore, in their unwavering commitment to excellence, they have the courage and determination to lead.

SMART

MANAGING

PERSONAL LEADERSHIP DEVELOPMENT
Each person within the organization has a capacity for incremental knowledge. It is in the organization's best interests to provide opportunities for all employees to learn and grow. Employees will not develop at the same pace or achieve the same level, of course, but all should be encouraged to develop their personal leadership skills to the fullest extent possible. Management has the responsibility to provide the environment and opportunities necessary to promote learning. Each employee has a responsibility to take advantage of those opportunities to achieve the highest levels of his or her capability. Personal leadership development is a core responsibility for managers within enlightened organizations.

Research on Mentoring

While mentoring also has quite a storied past, it has not been studied much until recently. Now, it appears to be attracting substantially more attention.

As evidenced by the substantial amount of research conducted in recent decades, mentoring is a topic of significance. Research suggests that mentoring is an important human resource management strategy.

There were two important studies conducted in the 1970s that acted as a catalyst for much of the current research on mentoring. Both of these research projects proposed that it was advantageous to an employee to have a mentor and beneficial to a manager to serve as a mentor. Employees moved into more desirable jobs and gained greater access to the power structures within their organizations and managers experienced rejuvenation of their careers.

Managers must value the mentoring process before they are able to function effectively as mentors. In some work environments, especially small- and medium-sized enterprises, leadership development is inhibited by the perception that workforce development, including mentoring, is of little or no value. This is due to a lack of evidence that clearly demonstrates the link between mentoring and profitability. For example, a detailed and systematic study of more than 1,640 small- and medium-sized enterprises over an eight-year period failed to find consistent links between training and development and a range of performance-related variables such as survival, sales growth, and profitability.

Some organizations fail to justify investing in mentoring because they are not achieving profitability. Ironically, these organizations may be failing to achieve profitability because they do not invest more in their people.

> **MENTORS SHARE WISDOM**
>
> "Wisdom can neither be bought nor sold. But it can be shared."
> —Caron Grainger, "Mentoring—Supporting Doctors at Work and Play," *British Medical Journal,* June 29, 2002
>
> SMART
> MANAGING

Some scholars have challenged the research results, attributing them to a weakness in the methodology. It's also been claimed that the number of variables in studying mentoring makes it problematic to draw any solid conclusion.

There is concern in some organizations that if their employees improve their knowledge and skills, they will become more marketable and leave for other organizations. Ironically, many employees leave for jobs elsewhere because they don't feel that their current employers offer enough opportunities for them to develop.

The implication for both policy and practice is that the key to coaching and mentoring success within small- and medium-sized businesses lies with the manager. Managers must be willing and able to engage in development intervention, whether coaching or mentoring.

Finally, it should be noted again that the distinctions are often blurred among supervision, mentoring, and individualized personnel development strategies, such as coaching. They are processes with a shared foundation. This is only natural, as there is overlap among their purposes, elements of study, and their competencies. Unfortunately, in organizations in which the distinctions are not understood, the need for mentoring may not be recognized or appreciated. It's also likely that more conflicts will arise in mentoring relationships. This will be a main theme of this chapter.

Four Factors of Mentoring

When the leaders of organizations recognize the value of investing in developmental intervention and when managers are willing and able to mentor, they should consider four factors:

1. alignment of objectives
2. shared expectations
3. dynamics of the mentoring relationship
4. positions and responsibilities

Alignment of Objectives

If the *organization* is to benefit from a mentoring relationship, that relationship must develop the employee so that he or she can contribute more toward helping the organization achieve its objectives. If the *employee* is to benefit from a mentoring relationship, the relationship must enable him or her to develop toward personal objectives in line with his or her career aspirations. It makes sense that the better the objectives of both parties are aligned, the more effective and efficient the mentoring can be. Obviously, when these objectives are less in alignment, the outcome will be less satisfactory.

CAVEAT MENTOR

When the objectives of both organization and employee are fully aligned and they share the same expectations, the conditions are most favorable for the mentor to work on behalf of both parties. However, when the parties are not in agreement on what they expect from mentoring, the mentor will be in a conflicted position. The smart mentor will work out compromises as necessary, but it may be wiser in that situation to bring the mentoring relationship to an end.

Shared Expectations

In mentoring as in most projects, the key to success is creating shared expectations, making sure that each party knows what to expect from the other. Shared expectations are critical to communicating, collaborating, coordinating, avoiding confusion, and minimizing conflict. The three parties—the organization, the employee being mentored, and the manager who is mentoring—should have a common understanding of what to expect from the mentoring relationship. It should be understood that the mentor is to be working on behalf of both the organization and the employee. If the mentor can balance the two "clients," there is less likely to be any conflict.

When the mentor works on behalf of the organization, there is a potential conflict with the mentee. Likewise, when the mentor works on behalf of the mentee, there is a potential conflict with the organization.

START WITH SHARED EXPECTATIONS

It is important for a mentoring relationship to begin with a common understanding of what the organization and the employee being mentored expect from the mentor. That understanding should be based on an alignment of the organization's objectives and the employee's personal career aspirations and goals. Shared expectations are the base from which the mentor and the protégé can work together most effectively and efficiently.

Dynamics of the Mentoring Relationship

This factor needs no explanation. Any human relationship is a mesh of personalities, attitudes, beliefs, interests, and so forth. Add to that the differences between the mentor and the protégé in terms of positions and responsibilities, knowledge, abilities, and experience. There are also issues intrinsic to the mentoring relationship. How well does the mentor teach? How well does the protégé learn? How well do they communicate? How sensitive are they to the fine points that can matter so much in any organization, particularly social aspects and "politics"?

Positions and Responsibilities

The fourth factor in mentoring relationships is positions and responsibilities—the current function of the manager and the current function of the employee. Put simply, an employee can be mentored either by his or her immediate manager or by a manager from another department or at a higher level.

Supervisor as Mentor

Let's begin with the fourth factor—positions and responsibilities. It may seem logical for employees to be mentored by the manager who supervises them. After all, he or she knows the employee's job responsibilities best and is most familiar with how well they are fulfilling those responsibilities. Also, the logistics would seem to favor this arrangement: employees generally spend most or all of their time at work closer to their supervisor than to other managers. It would be easiest to have managers mentor the employees they supervise.

DON'T TRY WEARING TWO HATS

Traditionally, employees use managers as mentors and coaches. They entrust their career development to them. However, the roles of manager and mentor are so fundamentally different that they are bound to conflict at some point in time. It makes sense to separate these roles more explicitly—ideally, to find someone else to serve as mentor.

Sadly, few organizations understand the differences between the two roles and they make no effort to resolve the inherent conflict. Moreover, they do not equip their managers to function as mentors or coaches effectively or prepare them to avoid conflicts or handle them when they arise.

Furthermore, the supervising manager has the position, power, and authority to help his or her employees most immediately, through choice assignments, performance rewards, and growth opportunities. This situation can give the employee a substantial advantage.

For all these reasons, it may seem logical and easiest for an employee to be mentored by his or her supervisor, but this arrangement is not generally the best situation. In fact, it should most often be avoided.

Managers organize and direct the work of their employees. Mentors inspire employees and encourage them to reach for higher levels of performance. While each function is important, managers and mentors have different responsibilities. When a manager serves as a mentor for his or her employees, the two roles and their responsibilities are likely to be in conflict.

There are several negatives associated with this situation.

A manager is responsible for the performance of each of his or her subordinates and the performance of the group. If he or she is mentoring one or some but not all of the members of that group, there are two possible ramifications. Those who are not in a mentoring relationship with their manager could feel at a disadvantage, in a way, like second-class citizens within the group, victims of favoritism. This may not be simply a feeling: a protégé may try to take advantage of becoming closer to the manager, expecting special treatment. Also, there could be a perception that the needs of individuals supersede the needs of the team.

DON'T ASSUME YOU CAN MENTOR

CAUTION

Just because you are successful at managing your employees does not necessarily mean that you will be successful in mentoring them. Again, managing and mentoring are not the same. As a manager, you are responsible for producing business results by effectively deploying all of your allocated resources. Your success will be determined based on the success of your team. You may get a feeling of satisfaction through your mentoring efforts and you may score points, but be careful that mentoring doesn't distract from managing.

Supervising usually entails assessing job performance. A manager who is mentoring a subordinate might find it difficult to remain objective about an employee he or she is helping develop, to separate the performance review by the supervisor from the support functions of a mentor. This situation might be more than uncomfortable; it could lead to a conflict of interest or at least the perception of a conflict by other employees and by higher-level managers. Both the mentor and the protégé could suffer from that eventuality.

If the supervisor-mentor and his or her protégé disagree on the performance assessment, there is an obvious potential for conflict. Yet when they agree on the performance assessment, there is potential for conflict. Whether the assessment is accurate or inaccurate is irrelevant for this discussion. The potential conflict does not develop because of a disagreement over the assessment, but rather because of the consequences associated with the outcome, relative to the new expectations of the organization and the mentee.

In addition, when a manager mentors a subordinate, he or she may feel threatened by the possible results of the mentoring. Several studies have shown that mentoring and protégé relationships do not evolve into positive relationships when the alliances involve individuals who have conflicting career needs.

For example, the protégé is ready to move on to greater responsibility and autonomy, while the mentor persists in wanting to provide direction: the manager may not actually want that employee to perform at a higher level. The manager could feel anxious about losing that employee when he or she develops to the point of being qualified to pursue opportunities outside that department; a manager could feel conflicted over what he or she wants and what the employee wants. The manager could even feel worried that the protégé could eventually displace him or her as manager of that department or perhaps compete for promotional and other opportunities.

Sometimes the conflict between the protégé's objectives and the supervisor-mentor's objectives may be interpreted as something larger. The protégé and/or other employees may believe that management in general does not support the career aspirations of employees.

There's also the possibility, maybe even probability, that all will not go smoothly. A manager who is mentoring a subordinate may feel uncomfortable dealing with the conflicts when they ultimately surface and it may be difficult to resolve them appropriately while wearing both hats.

Either the supervisor–subordinate relationship or the mentor–mentee relationship, maybe both, may be constrained. Furthermore, the mentoring is more likely to be short-lived because the manager must give priority to his or her supervisory responsibilities.

Most frequently, employees do not have the opportunity to select their manager. However, most often managers do have the option to select their employees. To be effective, employees should select the person who will mentor them. If they cannot select, employees should at least have the right to veto the prospective mentor if they are not comfortable with a mentor who may have been assigned to them. In general, most managers make the effort to try and align company goals with the personal career aspirations of their employees. However, as soon as some of the individual career aspirations begin to conflict, or are perceived to be in conflict, with the goals of the organization, many managers shy away from their mentoring activities.

Two Roles, Two Models

A mentor will often play a role or provide a service to the protégé that is not appropriate for the manager. The manager should concentrate on helping his or her employees improve their performance in the job and leave the mentoring to someone else. A mentor should be at least one level higher in the organization than the protégé and away from the immediate field of action.

Kathleen Gallacher identified three interventions—supervision, mentoring, and coaching, as methods for supporting personnel development (*Reforming Personnel Preparation in Early Intervention: Issues, Models, and Practical Strategies,* Baltimore: Paul H. Brookes Publishing, 1997, pp. 191–213). She described supervision as a broader scope, which incorporates administrative functions and entails performance evaluation. Further, she described mentoring as an informal process, more narrow in scope than supervision. She also suggests that although mentoring may be one strategy by which the organization accomplishes professional development and promotes assimilation of new employees, a supervisor typically is not an individual's mentor. On occasion, both a supervisor and a mentor may employ coaching in their work.

While all three forms of intervention should be viewed as constructive, supervision is more aligned with the typical responsibilities of management. The latter, mentoring intervention, is opportunity-driven and best supported by a mentor versus a manager.

Both the manager and the mentor should function as role models for the protégé. However, the manager should be more like a coach than a mentor and the mentor should be more like a partner and counselor than a manager. The manager should demonstrate the proficiency and skills that are necessary to perform the job in an outstanding manner. The mentor should demonstrate role model behavior by supporting the employee through encouragement and inspiration while setting meaningful and challenging personal career goals.

MANAGERS AS ROLE MODELS
Managers must learn the power of setting a great example. Effective role modeling has been shown to increase job satisfaction and improve overall performance. The results of leading by example are remarkable, but what compels managers to set the example is their desire to set the tone for others. Role models recognize that others want the opportunity to learn from their performance and behaviors. The extreme personal leader is a role model who does not wait for others to set the tone.

The manager should provide ongoing coaching and support, as well as training and development to help the employee continue to improve in his or her job. Meanwhile, the mentor should help socialize the protégé in environments that will prepare him or her for responsibilities beyond that current job.

I strongly recommend that managers partner with employees in the process of creating individual personal development plans. By doing so, managers have the opportunity to help employees define their specific personal needs and identify the best person who might be available and willing to serve as a mentor.

TRICKS OF THE TRADE

INFLUENCE THROUGH ATTITUDE
The successful career plan will include, of course, the basic work-related training, which develops knowledge and skills, but personal leadership ability and attitude are also fundamental to a comprehensive personal career plan. Enlightened managers recognize that organizations that achieve sustained, high levels of performance do so because of the outstanding performance and positive attitudes of their employees. Great skills are important, but what really drives employees to do exceptional things is the influence of attitude.

Other Manager as Mentor

It's generally wiser for an employee to have a mentor from outside his or her department. Such a mentor would not have the authority to manage the employee's work activity, but would lead by example by sharing his or her views and inspiring the protégé with his or her own vision and enthusiasm. This may be within a formal corporate mentoring program or as an informal mentoring process.

For mentoring to be most effective, the employee should select the person who will mentor him or her. If that's not possible and someone else makes the choice, the employee should at least have the right to veto the selection if he or she does not feel comfortable with that person.

What does it take to be a good mentor? To be successful as a mentor, I believe you must also be successful as a manager. Perhaps more important, I believe successful mentors also are effective leaders. Managers who demonstrate good leadership, managerial, and supervisory skills will be more effective in helping their protégés.

Potential Problems

Even when a manager and an employee are matched well as mentor and protégé, problems can arise. There are many factors that will determine the success or failure of a mentor–and–protégé relationship.

As mentioned earlier, it's important for the aspirations and objectives of the employee to be in alignment with the vision and objectives of the organization. That's the ideal start for an effective mentoring relationship. However, sometimes what the employee wants may conflict or seem to conflict with what's best for the organization. The employee may want something different or want to accelerate the development process.

If this happens, the mentoring manager may react and shy away from mentoring activities. As the shared expectations of the mentoring relationship change, the mentor can no longer be working on behalf of both the protégé and the organization. Thus, with this developing imbalance, we might see a conflict arise.

There can also be problems with the dynamics of the relationship. The two personalities may clash or simply not mesh very well. Communication may suffer. One or both parties may become impatient. Enthusiasm may wane. So many factors, both small and large, can affect the mentor–protégé relationship.

Think Carefully About Mentoring

So, with all the possibilities for problems, it is necessary to caution managers to think carefully and consider all the issues before taking on the responsibility of mentoring.

HELPING OUTSIDE

Managers should seek opportunities to serve as mentors for employees who work outside their immediate area of the organization. This will allow them the opportunity to expand their knowledge about the organization while providing inspiration and leadership support to employees outside their normal sphere of influence. They also may enjoy working one-on-one, more closely than they do in supervising. Mentoring will increase the manager's visibility and provide more opportunities for career development. Also, when employees see their supervisor going beyond job responsibilities to serve as a mentor, it will encourage them to do likewise.

The first question a manager should ask is whether he or she has the interest and passion for mentoring. If a manager does not have a passion for providing guidance and direction to help an employee pursue his or her personal career objectives, then it's better to avoid entering into any type of mentoring relationship.

The second question a manager should ask is whether he or she has the required capacities to really help the employee. Just because you are a manager does not mean you will be an effective mentor. So ask yourself, "Do I have the right skills and experiences that might be helpful to a particular individual seeking mentorship?"

The skills necessary to be an effective manager are important in developing and implementing an effective mentoring program. However, these skills alone are insufficient. Furthermore, even a manager who is an effective leader may still be somewhat deficient in the skills necessary to be an effective mentor.

One simple rule to keep in mind is the following: In general, managers direct, leaders inspire, and mentors guide. However, the most successful mentors do a little of each.

It is reasonable to expect that the manager and mentor should be working toward a common set of objectives. Both should strive to improve the overall effectiveness and efficiency of the organization. Both should view employees as the organization's pathway to success. They just play different roles.

Managers who strongly believe in developing employees are more likely to be successful as managers. However, just because managers believe in developing employees and are successful as managers does not mean they will be equally as successful at mentoring.

Managers can be effective mentors and mentors should be effective managers. However, it is very difficult for someone to effectively manage and mentor the same person. It takes a unique set of skills and experiences to do so.

Generally, in the best interest of the corporation and the individual, managers who have a desire to mentor individuals should seek mentees from outside of their immediate departments and organizations. Similarly, individuals, who are interested in being mentored, should look for a mentor other than their immediate supervisor.

The most effective managers learn how to lead and learn how to be a mentor. But even the most effective managers will always have an inherent conflict when they manage, lead, and mentor the same individual. It would certainly be a wonderful outcome if more managers were experienced enough and had the passion to do all three. However, it is highly unlikely that this will be common.

> **SMART MANAGING**
>
> ## Encouraging Outside Help
>
> Managers should encourage their employees to seek mentors outside of their organizations. As mentioned earlier, I advise managers against serving as mentors for their immediate employees. However, I strongly recommend that they help their employees develop individual personal development plans. By doing so, managers take the opportunity to help each employee who shows interest to define his or her specific personal needs and identify the best possible person who might be available and willing to serve as a mentor.

Hired Help

Managers should identify their high-potential and high-aspiration employees and seek mentors for them from outside their organization. Each manager is responsible for maintaining a current assessment of the strengths and weaknesses of his or her employees and for developing a strategic plan to minimize the weaknesses and capitalize on the strengths. When managers seek the best possible mentors for their employees, they should include individuals from outside their departments and outside their companies too.

MENTOR? COACH?

CAUTION People chosen to mentor employees from outside their area assume that the employees are performing in an outstanding manner. If an employee's current performance is less than outstanding, then he or she should be considering a coach instead of a mentor. Training and development for the sake of improving performance in the job is the responsibility of the employee's manager. Mentors may be able to affect employee performance through their influence, but it's not their responsibility.

Using a combination of inside and outside mentors to help develop their high-potential and high-aspiration employees will substantially improve the performance of their organization.

The mentor is responsible for providing the employee with insight, perspective, and inspiration that will encourage the individual to reach high enough to achieve his or her personal career objectives. Employees who are highly motivated to perform at their highest levels of capability will substantially increase productivity for the organization.

Organizations should make employee leadership development a collaborative responsibility of individual leaders, line managers, the human resources department, and, yes, mentors. If all the aforementioned people are engaged in the process of people development, the company and the individuals will benefit tremendously.

In the next chapter we will discuss the value of mentoring. In essence, we will answer the question: Who needs a mentor?

Manager's Checklist for Chapter 2

☑ Make sure your employees understand the differences between *managing* and *mentoring*.

☑ Do not mentor your own employees. Work with them to create individual personal development plans. Encourage your high-performance employees to seek a mentor. Coach employees who need help. But leave the mentoring to others.

☑ Consider mentoring an employee outside your area.

☑ Strive to maintain shared expectations.

Who Needs a Mentor?

The first two chapters have covered the basics of the what and the who of mentoring. In this chapter the focus is on the why. The easy answer is performance, but there's a lot more to it.

Mentoring for Top Performance and Leadership Succession

Top global companies encourage their high-potential employees to stretch themselves in ways that will prepare them for future opportunities. The leaders within these organizations believe personal relationships are key to developing their leaders. They take an active and personal interest in developing and preparing their next generation of leaders. Both informal and formal mentoring are considered important development strategies.

Top-performing companies maintain a vigilant commitment to leadership development. These organizations believe that people development is equally as important as product development. Leadership differentiates successful businesses from the unsuccessful ones. Organizations that maintain a supply of talented leaders are more effective. Not surprisingly, leadership development is given a far higher priority at top global companies. According to a study ("The 2007 Top Companies for Leaders," Hewitt Associates and The RBL Group, *Fortune,* October 1, 2007), 85 percent of the top global companies believe the organization currently has the talent pipeline

SMART MANAGING

PEOPLE PIPELINE

Enlightened managers understand and value the succession planning processes necessary to ensure they have the appropriate mix of personnel skills required to execute their management responsibilities. Managers must build and maintain a pipeline of talent that flows through the succession planning process efficiently. Personnel resources must be developed such that the appropriate skills are available to management as they are needed. Therefore, management must plan for unanticipated and planned changes in the organization that will affect their pipeline.

CAUTION

DON'T RISK YOUR COMPANY OR YOUR CAREER

When managers fail to invest in developing their people, they risk the failure of their company and, most likely, jeopardize their careers. Managers must be willing to take risks on their people in order to minimize the risk to their companies. If you fail to invest in your people today, they are likely to be less productive and less valuable to you in the future.

necessary to be successful in the future. In contrast, only 42 percent of all other companies believe they have the necessary talent pipeline. In essence, the top companies understand the need for mentors, value the services provided by mentors, and encourage the relationships.

According to another study conducted by Hewitt Associates a few years ago, 76 percent of the *Fortune* 25 corporations were offering mentoring programs. In contrast, only 55 percent of less successful companies were offering mentoring programs. In fact, 71 percent of *Fortune* 500 companies were using mentoring to ensure that people were held accountable to their commitment to learning. Further, 75 percent of the executives in this study stated that mentoring played a key role in their career success. Specifically, mentoring was one of three factors influencing the career success of CEOs at *Fortune* 500 companies ("100 Best Companies to Work For," *Fortune*, January 10, 2000, cited by Barry Sweeny, *www.businessmentorcenter.com*).

Mentoring for Knowledge

Today, forward-thinking organizations recognize that mentoring is an effective way to develop intellectual capital to remain competitive. Leading organizations consider mentoring a knowledge transfer strategy. The driving force in a mentoring relationship is the learning process. The effectiveness of that process comes from the dynamics and quality of the relationship.

Many organizations include promotions and compensation as part of their employee retention strategy. As a result, employees are frequently rewarded with management and executive-level positions without substantial experience. When organizations provide mentoring to these employees during their transitions, they minimize the risk to the organization while helping the employees learn the ropes and develop the on-site knowledge, skills, and behaviors necessary to perform effectively in their new positions.

Mentoring Is a Personal Business

Mentoring is an interpersonal relationship that is built on trust. It is viewed as a safe place where mentees can be open and free to share their true personal career aspirations without being threatened for thinking too boldly. Some of the more powerful people in the world have depended on advice and mentoring, from CEOs of *Fortune* 500 companies to heads of state, including the current president of the United States, Barack Obama.

As discussed in a previous chapter, mentoring is not a new phenomenon. However, the broad understanding and applicability of mentoring

MAKE SURE PEOPLE KNOW YOU

There are ongoing debates that suggest that *what* you know is more important than *whom* you know. Whom you know is less important than it is purported to be and what you know is often irrelevant unless you know someone who needs what you know or cares about the subject. Actually, although both questions are important, neither is as important as this one: Who knows you?

The fact that you know someone is substantially less valuable than who knows you. For example, many people may know Warren Buffett, but receive little value from that connection. On the other hand, those individuals who are known by Buffet are in a better position to benefit from their relationship. So, rather than flaunting whom they know, managers should be striving to do things that earn them the right to be known by other people.

programs only began to surface during the 18th and 19th centuries. This was the direct result of informative literature that targeted young people who demonstrated a passion for learning and high potential. Consequently, career-oriented individuals have conceptualized the idea that capitalizing on the deep knowledge and the guidance of others, such as mentors, will help accelerate their careers.

In fact, there is substantial data to support this thesis. Researchers have argued that career advancement, increased earning power, improved employee satisfaction, and reductions in employee attrition are all directly attributed to successful mentoring programs.

The Mentoring Network

Any employee who has high aspirations and high potential needs a mentor. It can be an excellent way to get help developing skills and competencies from someone he or she trusts, learning from the experiences of the mentor through the transfer of knowledge. The mentee also builds confidence and expands his or her professional network.

> **TRICKS OF THE TRADE**
>
> **NETWORKING**
>
> Effective mentors always find opportunities to broaden the exposure of their mentees to people of relative power and influence. Networking is a proven way to effectively expose mentees to individuals who are in positions to influence the velocity of the mentee's personal career plans.
>
> However, the best mentors do more than provide exposure for their protégés. They go beyond the typical round-robin meetings where finger food is served and business cards are exchanged. These mentors provide their mentees with visibility and the opportunity to meet individually with prominent people who can help change their lives.

Choosing a Mentor

Choosing a mentor can be one of the most important steps in an employee's professional life. It is likely that some employees may have many mentors during different phases of their career. In fact, at times they may have more than one mentor. An employee could have a mentor from work, a mentor from within his or her profession or industry, and a professional mentor. Each of these mentors could provide the employee with a unique set of experiences that are valuable for his or her career advancement.

While a mentee may increase his or her skills, build confidence, and expand his or her network, these activities only provide a baseline for an effective mentoring relationship. To build on this foundation, the mentee must clearly define specific goals for career and personal advancement.

Career Stages and Reasons to Have a Mentor

There are several stages in a career when mentoring is more likely to be considered.

For new employees joining the firm with a limited amount of experience, mentoring could be used effectively to accelerate their integration into the organization. In this scenario, a mentoring relationship might be equally as attractive to the employee as to the organization. Of course, as discussed earlier, this will not always be the case.

Employees who are approaching the middle of their career can also benefit from having a mentor. In some cases a mentor may inspire the employee to revitalize energy and excitement that is necessary to improve his or her long-term career opportunities. Managers may provide mentoring because they believe it is necessary to retain the talent and/or because they feel the need to accelerate the development of the employee.

Employees who are nearing the end of their career could benefit from mentoring, as well. They are likely to seek a mentoring relationship to help them define a plan and a strategy for pursuing new career options outside their current work environment. At times, management will provide a mentor to help employees make a successful transition outside the company. It may be the direct result of clearing the way for new talent within the organization or it could simply be that the employee has expressed interest to move on to some other endeavor.

An employee may seek a mentor at any point simply to receive guidance regarding many career opportunities perceived to be available. Another reason could simply be that the employee does not believe that his or her career is progressing at an acceptable pace. Employees who have been successful are likely to have experienced a mentoring relationship during their career and recognize that they will require additional support to take their career advancement to the next level.

EVERYONE IS A TOAD ON A FENCE POST

FOR EXAMPLE

I vividly recall enjoying with my wife the pleasure of dining in Flint, Michigan with Alex Haley, the late and famed author of *Roots: The Saga of an American Family*, more than two decades ago. During our dinner conversation, I asked Mr. Haley how he had achieved his success as an author.

Haley replied by asking me, "Have you ever seen a toad sitting on the top of a fence post in the middle of a field?" I reminded him, trying to be a bit humorous, that I had grown up in the suburbs of Chicago, so the obvious answer was "No."

After a short pause, Mr. Haley looked at me and said, "Wherever you are, if you ever see a toad sitting on the top of a fence post in the middle of a field, you will know that it had to have some help in getting there. And I am just a toad."

The moral of this story is that we are all just toads.

In each of the scenarios discussed, the need for a mentor could be equally important. In fact, all people, at some point in their careers, will need a little help. Anyone who seeks the opportunity to learn, grow, and advance his or her career will need help in the process. It is incredibly naïve for someone to assume that he or she can succeed in building a successful career without assistance.

Three Ways to Succeed

There are only three honorable ways to achieve personal career success in business.

First, employees can be exceptionally lucky and always be in the right place at the right time and do all of the right things for the right people. While some luck is necessary and should be expected, it should not be the foundation of any employee's personal career plan. Serendipity should never be used as a substitute for hard work and preparation.

Second, employees may be blessed and gifted in such a way that their talents and skill sets are far superior to those of anyone else in their organizations. They may prepare through hard work, build the right relationships within their organizations, and earn the opportunity to advance their careers.

Some people may be fortunate to work for organizations that offer them an inherent competitive advantage. For example, in a family business, members of the family may be entitled to inherit leadership. Or in a corporation that has more limited talent and resources, an employee could easily stand out through his or her contributions. Fortunately, most corporations have ready access to sufficient talent pools such as exist in most industries. However, in some rare, limited situations an employee may evolve as one of a kind.

The third way of achieving personal career success in business is through hard work, preparation, and guidance. Effective mentors provide employees with this guidance. As discussed in a previous chapter, preparation is the key to success. Without preparation there is no knowledge, without knowledge there is no power, and without power there is no way to succeed in business. Power, in the form of knowledge, is meaningless unless it is earned and shared throughout the organization. A mentor will help the employee learn how to earn the power to influence outcomes within the organization.

> **KNOW WHEN TO LEAVE**
>
> There's a positive correlation between having aspirations and potential and needing a mentor. Plato had Socrates, Tom Peters had Peter Drucker, and Luke Skywalker had Obi-Wan Kenobi. Even Tiger Woods has a coach. However, as in any relationship, a mentoring arrangement can change over time. If the relationship becomes too personal or if the mentee begins relying less and less on the mentor's advice, it might be time to find a new mentor (Amy Barrett, "Why You Need a Mentor," *BusinessWeek*, Winter 2007).

Mentors are not people who only tell you what you want to hear. While mentors should encourage and applaud the success of their mentees, their real value is in the objective and honest advice that they provide. But just because everyone can benefit from a mentor does not suggest that everyone is ready to enter into a mentoring relationship.

Mentors offer substantial value to individuals who want to accelerate their progress toward their personally defined career objectives. Only those persons who have high aspirations to achieve something significant need mentors. Mentoring should be reserved for those employees who are doing something great or are in the pursuit of doing something great.

In the corporate world, mentoring is serious business and therefore it should be used only to link individual personal aspirations with the anticipated improved performance of the organization. Managers have the responsibility to identify those individuals who could benefit substantially from a mentoring program. They must seek out those individuals who demonstrate a potential for career advancement as well as opportunities to improve their performance in the current job.

Mentors Are Not Surrogate Coaches

As discussed in a prior chapter, all employees should benefit from on-the-job coaching. Sometimes the coaching may be provided by the immediate manager. Other times, since coaching is an intervention process, it may be more appropriate or effective if the coaching comes from someone other than the immediate manager.

If the employee needs coaching to improve his or her performance in the current job, but the long-term growth potential, as assessed by management, is limited, this person might benefit more from a coach than a mentor. Conversely, if management believes the employee has high-potential growth opportunities, then the coaching should be provided in the context of a mentoring program. Remember: Coaches provide only coaching support, but mentors can provide coaching within a mentoring program.

Earning the opportunity to be mentored is a privilege. However, mentoring should not be reserved only for those with high potential and high aspirations. All employees should be encouraged to seek mentoring as they deem appropriate.

To Be (Mentored) or Not to Be

So who needs a mentor? While every employee should consider whether he or she would like to be mentored, it is not necessary for everyone to be mentored. As a matter of fact, it is not in the best interest of the organization for each employee to be mentored. (Again, remember that mentoring is not coaching.)

Perhaps every employee could benefit from mentoring, just as perhaps every employee could benefit from coaching. However, while all should have the benefit of being coached to improve his or her performance as necessary, the same is not true for mentorship. As discussed in an earlier chapter, coaching and mentoring both are defined as intervention processes. Coaching intervention is necessary when an employee is not performing at the level expected. On the other hand, mentoring as an intervention process is more likely to be afforded only to those individuals who demonstrate an interest in advancing their careers or who have been identified as individuals with high potential who should be groomed and developed for more significant roles in the organization.

While all employees could benefit from having a mentor, it is not necessary and maybe not wise for the organization to provide a mentor to each of them. It is very likely that employees within an organization or a unit will have similar career aspirations. Therefore, if all of them were mentored, the result could be greater competition and conflicts among employees. Coaching for better performance, on the other hand, is less likely to cause a conflict because each member of the team would benefit more directly from the improved performance of his or her teammates.

I believe that every person within the organization should be considered for participation in a mentoring program, however, they must earn the opportunity to be selected. I do not believe that anyone has an entitlement to participate in a mentoring program. Like most things in life that are worth having, each individual must earn the opportunity to participate.

In certain situations, management will determine who will be mentored. At times, however, management will not determine who will be mentored. An individual employee may seek out a mentor from within the company without the knowledge of his or her immediate supervisor. It is also likely that employees will seek mentors from outside the corporation. In these two scenarios, managers should be concerned if they discover their employees are being mentored and they were unaware of the relationship. This is because the manager will miss out on the opportunity to partner with the employee in order to gain the maximum benefit from his or her mentor.

In some situations, an employee may pursue a mentor without his or her immediate manager's knowledge because he or she does not have the support of that manager. That might be the direct result of constructive dialogue that has taken place between the manager and the employee or it might be the result of a lack of constructive dialogue between them. However, it is certainly acceptable, and it should be expected, that employees will pursue their own career-advancement paths with or without management support.

The most ideal scenario is where the manager and the employee are working together to help the employee achieve his or her personal objectives. When managers are effectively engaged with their employees, they will recognize when an employee needs coaching. Enlightened managers will also understand and value their employees' need for mentoring. The employees should earn mentoring opportunities because of their job performance, high aspirations, and long-term potential as assessed by the organization.

So, whether an employee needs mentoring and could benefit from it is determined by the mentor, the immediate manager, and the employee. They could arrive at that conclusion together or independently. What management believes in this matter is less important than what the employee believes. If they disagree, the decision should always go to the employee.

However, just because the employee believes that he or she should have a mentor does not mean that the manager has to provide one. Regardless of whether management supplies a mentor, the immediate manager should make a reasonable effort to support the employee's initiative. Lois J. Zachary, author of *The Mentor's Guide: Facilitating Effective Learning Relationships*, provides an ecological viewpoint to describe mentoring: "Ecologists tell us that a tree planted in a clearing of an old forest will grow more successfully than one planted in an open field. The reason, it seems, is that the roots of the forest tree are able to follow the intricate pathways created by former trees and thus embed themselves more deeply. Similarly, human beings thrive best when we grow in the presence of those who have gone before. Our roots may not follow every available pathway, but we are able to become more fully ourselves because of the presence of others."

To some degree, all individuals within the organization need some form of mentoring. So perhaps the question is not who needs mentoring, but what type of mentoring is most appropriate for a particular individual.

10 WAYS TO USE A MENTOR

Jacqui Love Marshall reminds us that as teenagers we could get guidance from our parents, teachers, relatives, and other adults, but as we become adults we usually no longer have those sources of counsel. That's why we need mentors. She offers this top-10 list of benefits of mentors:

SMART

MANAGING

1. A learning partner
2. A confidential sounding board
3. A nonjudgmental counselor
4. A navigator, one who knows the ropes
5. A "Mr. or Ms. T" (for "truth"), someone to provide a reality check
6. A champion for your cause
7. A coach to shore up your weaknesses
8. A facilitator to broaden your networks and perspectives
9. A promise keeper, someone who holds you accountable
10. A guide to help you see beyond the horizon

("10 Reasons Why You Need a Mentor," *Fusion Magazine*, Spring 2005, www.naa.org)

Research has substantiated that mentoring is an excellent way to accelerate the development of high-potential employees. Still, mentoring programs should also be made available to those individuals who demonstrate an interest to earn increased responsibilities within their organizations. In some professions, such as teaching, medicine, and others, some form of mentoring is required for all employees entering the field. These mentoring programs are mandatory to ensure that the new professional is adequately prepared to assume a solo role in that profession.

Organizations should be interested in mentoring to accelerate the development of their employees and minimize the turnover rate. There is a double incentive for providing mentorship to your high-performing employees. If you provide them with effective mentoring, their performance will be further accelerated. Furthermore, mentoring will not only inspire those individuals to do better, but also encourage them to provide some level of mentoring to others within the organization. So the residual value from investing in your higher-performing employees trickles down throughout the entire organization. In other words, investing in a mentoring program for some employees in the organization will benefit the whole organization.

TAKE THE RISK TO AVOID THE WORST

If managers value their employees, they are willing to invest in them. In fact, they will do so if they value only their organization. As Zig Ziglar has pointed out, "The only thing worse than investing in your people and losing them is not investing in them and keeping them."

It has been shown that the cost of developing current employees is substantially less expensive than the cost of hiring people to replace employees who feel neglected and decide to pursue appreciation of their talents elsewhere. Mentoring should play a major role in organizations that value developing their people.

Now that we know who needs a mentor, let's move on to the next chapter and discuss what we should expect from the mentor. We will define what the mentor should expect to provide to the mentee and what the mentee should expect to receive from a mentor. Managers should understand their roles in mentoring. Remember: Managers should expect what they get.

Manager's Checklist for Chapter 3

☑ Build and maintain a system for developing your people, to prepare for planned and unanticipated changes in the organization.

☑ Strive to do things that earn you the right to be known by other people. Whom you know and what you know are less important than who knows you.

☑ Find opportunities to help any employees you're mentoring to meet people of relative power and influence who can help change their lives.

☑ Help any of your employees who are being mentored or seeking a mentor to clearly define their specific goals for career and personal advancement.

☑ Assume your responsibility for identifying employees who could benefit substantially from a mentoring program. Seek out those individuals who demonstrate a potential for career advancement as well as opportunities to improve their performance in the current job.

☑ Promote the trickle-down benefits of mentoring in your organization. Provide effective mentoring to not only help high-performing employees develop further and faster and inspire them to do better, but also to encourage them to provide mentoring to others.

☑ Remember: "The only thing worse than investing in your people and losing them is not investing in them and keeping them."

What to Expect From a Mentor

I n this chapter we will concentrate on the needs of the mentee. We will discuss what mentees should expect from their mentors. When managers view the mentoring process from the eyes of the mentees, they are likely to better understand the mentees' needs. In addition, when necessary, managers should be able to more effectively respond to issues and concerns that may arise during the relationship.

This chapter is written as if it were addressed to an employee interested in being mentored, rather than to you as a manager. It is intended to give you a realistic sense of the perspective from the other side of the mentoring equation.

What Do You Want? What Do You Need?

To partner with a mentor effectively, you must first determine general expectations—what you expect from yourself and what you expect from the individual you will be selecting to be your professional mentor.

When seeking a mentor, you must make every effort to select someone who is best prepared to help you attain your professional goals. Therefore, before you start defining what you expect from a mentor and before you identify the mentor with whom you want to work, it's important that you allocate substantial time to define your needs, your career objectives, and your expectations for yourself.

When you know what you want and what you need, then you will be able to match your requirements more effectively with people who are available to mentor you. For example, if you desire to move into the senior ranks of the accounting profession, it seems obvious that you should at least consider someone who has either experience as a senior professional in the accounting profession or at least direct relationships with individuals within that profession who may be able to help you.

On the other hand, while it may not seem intuitive, you may also want to consider someone who has experience in dealing with senior executives, but not necessarily very deep connections in the accounting profession. In other words, I do not believe it is necessary for the mentor to come from the same background as the mentee.

WHAT DO MENTORS DO?

FOR EXAMPLE

"The best response to the question 'What do mentors do?' may be 'It depends.' Mentors may be thought of as teachers. They may develop their protégé's intellectual and career skills. They model, inform, confirm or disconfirm, prescribe, or question. Mentors may also act as sponsors, assisting protégés in developing and sharing their own network of personal contacts. They protect, promote, and support. Mentors may act as counselors, providing advice, guidance, moral support, and nurturing. They listen, probe, clarify, and advise. The mentor may act simply as a host or guide, sharing an informal social network with the protégé. Mentors may serve as exemplars. The mentor may provide a standard of excellence that the protégé will aspire to surpass." ("Mentoring for the New Millennium," William O. Walker, Patrick C. Kelly, and Roderick F. Hume, Jr., *Medical Education Online*, 2002; 7:15)

What Should You *Not* Expect From a Mentor?

While it is important to define what you expect from yourself and your mentor, it is equally important to understand what you should *not* expect from a mentor.

First and foremost, you should not expect your mentor to be your manager. Why not? Because your manager can give you a salary increase and promote you—and your manager can fire you or at least cause you to be fired. It's better if your mentor is not in a position to directly cause your employment to be terminated. Only in some rare situations should an employee's supervisor also be his or her mentor.

The person you choose to be your mentor most likely will never give you a raise in pay. However, if you select the right mentor and form a good partnership, you should be earning raises more frequently and those increases are likely to be more substantial.

Also, you should not expect your mentor to be your coach. In some cases, a mentor may also provide some coaching support. But a mentor's role is substantially different from the role of a coach. Hire a coach if you are seeking assistance in improving your on-the-job performance. Seek a mentor if you are striving to achieve high-aspiration objectives. While both reasons for seeking assistance are important, they are certainly not the same. Improving on-the-job performance is usually a condition of continued employment. However, striving for excellence in pursuit of high-aspiration goals is most often optional.

Certainly, you should not necessarily expect your mentor to be your personal friend. In some cases, it is acceptable for mentees to become friends with their mentors. However, in other situations, it might hinder the mentee from achieving his or her stated objectives.

It may seem to be somewhat of a contradiction, but friends are often the last to tell you what you most need to know. Because they value your relationship, they may be reluctant to challenge you or risk offending you.

Well, effective mentors know that the truth hurts. That is why great mentors are willing to inflict pain through honest evaluation when it is in the best interest of their mentees. Do not allow yourself to be confused. What you need is a mentor, not a friend.

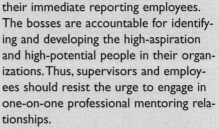

THE BOSS IS SELDOM RIGHT

As established earlier, rarely should supervisors mentor their immediate reporting employees. The bosses are accountable for identifying and developing the high-aspiration and high-potential people in their organizations. Thus, supervisors and employees should resist the urge to engage in one-on-one professional mentoring relationships.

Supervisors have a responsibility to encourage and support their employees in their pursuit of career advancement. In this regard, they should help employees find the appropriate mentors. However, they do not need to serve as best friends or mentors. Mentors should not be in positions to directly cause employees to be terminated.

Trust, Honesty, and Integrity

Some of the basic expectations of a mentor should include honesty and integrity. These two qualities form the basis for trust.

Trust

Trust is a relationship of reliance. Certainly, all expectations outlined in this chapter are important. However, trust trumps them all. Trust should be the basic foundation for most relationships. You must trust your mentor.

This is the cornerstone for establishing and maintaining your mentoring relationship. You should demand confidentiality. Satisfaction with a mentoring relationship is highly dependent on the interaction between the mentor and the mentee. You should expect your mentor to be open and candid with you. Otherwise, it will be difficult or at least unwise to trust him or her.

Your mentor should also be able to trust you, of course.

> **TRUST IS THE FOUNDATION**
>
> Trust demands zero tolerance. According to Ralph E. Viator ("An Analysis of Formal Mentoring Programs and Perceived Barriers to Obtaining a Mentor at Large Public Accounting Firms," *Accounting Horizons*, 13, 1999), "a critical factor for building a mentoring relationship is that both mentor and mentee establish a sense of trust and commitment." Quite simply, according to John C. Maxwell, in *Mentoring 101*, "Trust is the single most important factor in building personal and professional relationships."

In the mentoring partnership, each partner should trust the other and prove worthy of being trusted.

Honesty

It would seem obvious to expect your mentor to be honest. However, I believe it's important that you understand the distinction between *honesty* and *intellectual honesty*.

A mentor must demonstrate a willingness to seek the opportunity to tell the truth. Of course you should always expect your mentor to be honest with you. However, you will benefit substantially more from your relationship if your mentor consistently provides honest feedback and information.

A mentor should not only tell the truth in answering the questions you ask. A mentor who seeks the opportunity to tell the truth will constantly provide you truthful information to answer questions that you should be asking.

During my career, I have always looked for opportunities to provide truthful information to the people with whom I have had the privilege of working. Rather than wait for colleagues, clients, or employees to raise questions that I anticipate, I see a responsibility to tell them what they may need or want to know, even before they ask. You should expect your mentor to tell you things that you want to know, in addition to what you need to know. Once again, you should expect your mentor to consistently seek opportunities to tell you the truth.

Honesty Commitment to the truth.

KEY TERM

This word implies a refusal to lie, steal, or deceive in any way. Managers must have an uncompromising regard for the acceptable standard for their environment. They should avoid selective disclosure and seek opportunities to tell people everything they need to know and some of the things they just want to know. However, managers are not required to tell everyone they know everything they know.

SMART

FRIEND OR MENTOR

Friendship is never a substitute for mentorship. Effective mentors value the need for truth. That's why they are willing to risk offending through honest evaluation when it's in the best interest of the mentee. Most friends are generally unwilling to be painfully honest. However, friends who care and are willing to show it can function as effective mentors. Typically, the stronger the friendship, the weaker the mentoring relationship will be, and vice versa.

MANAGING

I'd like to point out the distinction between *honesty* and *intellectual honesty*. Again we all should expect honesty of the people with whom we have the privilege of working. We can term this *social* honesty. However, with a mentor you should demand *intellectual* honesty as well. You should reciprocate accordingly. Expect a mentor to be honest, but demand that your mentor be as intellectually honest with you as you are with him or her.

Again, it's very important that you have realistic expectations. The more you expect from your mentor, the more your mentor will expect

Intellectual honesty Conscientiously probing one's understanding of

KEY TERM reality, pursuing the truth, living in alignment with one's beliefs, values, and understanding of reality. This concept is the introspective analysis of your view of the truth. It stresses the importance of a rigorous and respectful thought process. Truth and trust are at the core of all mentoring relationships. It is important for the mentor and mentee to share an open perspective relative to emotion and fact throughout their constructive dialogue.

THE MENTEE IS THE CUSTOMER

Mentors must understand that they work for their mentees. Before they try to define what they expect from their mentees, they must have a general idea of what their mentees expect of themselves.

The mentee is responsible for determining clear expectations for himself or herself. The mentor's role is to help the mentee realize career goals. Understandably, the mentee's goals must be linked to the success of the organization, too, as discussed in the first two chapters.

from you. If you expect your mentor to help you, then you must be prepared to build a very open and honest relationship with him or her. The more you give to your mentor, the more you will receive in return.

Integrity

The decisions that you and your mentor should use to drive toward your personal goals will be effective only if these decisions are grounded in facts. Good, factual information is the foundation of your success. You both must insist on exchanging information openly. Once you've established that you're both willing to exchange critical, factual information, the relationship will begin to flourish.

The open exchange of information is the catalyst for creating new opportunities to tell the truth and to hear the truth. In other words, ambiguity exists only momentarily and achieving clarity is recognized as a triumph.

You should expect your mentor, in addition to being intellectually honest with you at all times, to maintain the highest levels of integrity throughout your relationship. This means honoring his or her commitments at all times. It means providing you with direct constructive feedback.

If you want your mentor to act with integrity, you must show that you always act with integrity. That means no duplicity, no inconsistency with what you value and believe.

> **Integrity** Consistent and firm commitment to living according to one's values. Integrity has been **KEY TERM** described as doing what is right even when there are no witnesses. It is the moral compass.

It is important to be mindful that integrity is a concept based on a set of accepted norms in a given culture. Equally as important as having a common understanding of integrity between yourself and your mentor, is to have a commonly accepted way of measuring it. For example, a conventional way of defining *integrity* is honoring the commitments one makes. If your mentor tells you that he or she is going to do something, then you are entitled to expect that it will be done. However, I believe it is reasonable to understand that things do change and situations do evolve.

You should expect your mentor to be incapable of being corrupted. The relationship that you have with a mentor must be a personal one and the integrity of that relationship is paramount. You should expect integrity at the highest level at all times. There should be no room for error. Integrity is absolute—at least within the context of being a concept based on a set of accepted norms in a given culture.

One reason that trust is important is that you or your mentor will be reluctant to share critically important information unless both believe that the other is dealing with sincerity. Without trust, you are most likely to be too self-protective, resulting in a defensive posture that is sure to limit the effectiveness of the partnership.

Achieving high-aspiration goals requires mentees and mentors alike to accept unconventional ideas and participate in new types of learning activities. Positive results will be achieved only when a culture of trust prevails. The key to establishing a culture of trust is specificity, not ambiguity. The real issues and concerns must be fully exposed and fully explored.

Of course, to fully expose and fully explore real issues and concerns, it's important to respect constructive questions that probe the why, where, how, when, and what of every decision and circumstance, regard-

TRICKS OF THE TRADE

"PUT THE MOOSE ON THE TABLE"
Randall Tobias created this metaphor, which he explains in the opening pages of his book, *Put the Moose on the Table: Lessons in Leadership from a CEO's Journey Through Business and Life* (Indiana University Press, 2003). He imagines a moose in the room, like the traditional elephant that all present try to ignore. He suggests using his phrase to make a suggestion: "Let's address this issue as openly and as honestly as we would feel compelled to do if we had a real live moose to confront." He adds, "Somehow, describing an issue in that way seems to make people feel more comfortable in speaking as openly as they know how."

The mentee and mentor must be willing to "put the moose on the table" when they own it and they must have the courage and confidence to call for it when they suspect someone is trying to hide one in the room. There is insufficient space to accommodate a "moose" in a mentoring relationship.

less of the source. To achieve your personal goals, both questions and answers must be specific, not vague.

Availability

When selecting a mentor, you should seek someone who has adequate time to devote to your personal aspirations and be able to meet with you on a regular schedule. These regularly scheduled sessions should include in-person meetings and telephonic/videoconference meetings. You should meet with your mentor at least once or twice each month. However, during the early stages of the mentoring relationship, you should meet more frequently. In addition, you should meet as the need arises, of course.

The beginning sessions should be in person and last at least one hour. Remember: the more time you and your mentor invest at the beginning of the relationship, the more likely you are to achieve your personal objectives. Clarity of objectives is important and it takes time to achieve it.

In general, each meeting should last at least 30 minutes. Again, brief meetings should be scheduled as needed. Once the schedule has been set, your mentor should work diligently to adhere to the plan. With the exception of real emergencies, it should be a rare occasion that a meeting time must be changed.

You have an obligation to work with your mentor to schedule meeting times that are mutually acceptable. Work with your mentor to capture as much time and knowledge as he or she is willing and capable of delivering. Remember: This is a partnership.

You should anticipate your mentor will have several other commitments. If your prospective mentor is busy, you have selected a potential winner. Usually the persons who are doing mentoring are in positions to be mentors because they have been successful in

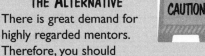

BUSY IS BETTER THAN THE ALTERNATIVE
There is great demand for highly regarded mentors. Therefore, you should expect them to be exceptionally busy. If the person you're considering selecting is not very busy and not retired, he or she is most likely the wrong person. In other words, a busy mentor is much more valuable than someone who is not.

However, just because the person you select as your mentor is busy, that is no excuse for not having time to execute his or her mentoring responsibilities. Therefore, it is important that the mentoring relationship be based on shared expectations regarding schedules and commitments.

their careers. Therefore, most mentors will be fully engaged in activities that keep them involved, or at least in touch, with those who will benefit your relationship. In other words, mentors are usually very busy people.

Nonetheless, you still should expect your mentor to schedule the appropriate time to work with you to achieve your objectives. It is also important that you demonstrate your commitment to achieving your personal goals by ensuring that you allocate sufficient time to meet with your mentor so that you have the opportunity to gain the maximum benefit from the relationship.

As discussed above, your mentor should be willing to commit to a schedule that is mutually acceptable to the both of you. You should expect him or her to meet with you as frequently as possible and to schedule other ways of communicating and meeting with you on a regular basis. Mentoring must be consistent. That means meeting at regular intervals to ensure that there is a steady flow of information between the two of you regarding the progress that you are making toward achieving your stated objectives. In other words, you should expect your mentor to be reliable and consistently available.

Effectiveness

One of the more important characteristics that you should expect from your mentor is effectiveness. How effective has your mentor been in achieving his or her own personal objectives? How successful has he or she been? How successful have his or her other mentees been? You determine what yardstick to use.

Does your mentor provide any support tools or programs to be used to assess your progress toward achieving your goals? How will you know where you are at any given time in the program? The answer to such questions may help you evaluate the effectiveness of the mentor.

As you can imagine, it will be somewhat difficult to personally assess how effective you believe your mentor will be before you begin the relationship. Nonetheless, this is very important to assess before you enter into an agreement with a mentor.

DELUSION

Remember: Just because someone is successful as a manager does not necessarily mean he or she will be effective as a mentor. Successful management skills do not directly mirror or translate into all the prerequisite skills necessary to be a successful mentor. Further, just because someone believes in mentoring, that does not qualify him or her as a mentor.

While passion and attitude are important, they are not sufficient preparation. To be successful, mentors must possess good management skills and great leadership qualities, which they have demonstrated consistently over time, as well as appropriate experiences.

It is important that you ascertain whether you believe this potential mentor will be effective in helping you. Although he or she may have been very effective in mentoring other individuals, I believe every mentoring relationship should be unique. Therefore, you should not assume that a mentor who has been effective with other mentees will be equally effective with you.

What is more important than relationships with other mentees is the relationship that you believe would develop between you and a potential mentor. Therefore the selection process involves assessing the potential of the interaction. The effectiveness of your mentor will be determined substantially by the personality match.

Expertise

You should expect your mentor to be exceptionally well qualified. In other words, he or she should demonstrate substantial subject matter expertise in a profession or industry that would help you most. Your mentor should have a record of success and be well respected by other leaders in his or her profession. Your mentor should be very good at what he or she does and that excellence should be substantiated by peers.

I will continue to stress that expertise is important. However, as mentioned early in this chapter, I also want to emphasize that it is not necessary that the mentor's expertise be in the exact area as your aspirations.

For example, if you are in engineering, you could be very successful partnering with someone who is in accounting, if he or she is effective as a mentor. You should not assume that a successful engineer is necessarily the best mentor for someone in engineering or a successful accountant would be the best mentor for someone in accounting. The success of the mentor is not necessarily determined by his or her specific job experiences.

For example, if you aspire to be a senior executive, with responsibility for sales and marketing, but you currently work in accounting, you might be better positioned with a mentor from the sales and marketing functions within your organization. The move from accounting to sales and marketing might put you in a better position to compete for broader career advancement opportunities. Again, as illustrated by this example, partnering with a mentor from your own profession will not necessarily be in your best interest.

When selecting a mentor, you must always be strategic in your thinking. You should analyze what expertise you will need and select your mentor accordingly.

CLARITY

Mentors must foster regular interactions with their mentees. They should help mentees establish, and maintain, a set of well-defined objectives. These goals should be measurable and achievable. When mentee and mentor agree on the desired outcomes of their relationship, they will be well aligned and there should be very little room for ambiguity.

Relevant Experience

You should expect substantial relevant experience from your mentor. As discussed earlier, "relevant experience" does not mean that the person has worked in the same industry or the same profession as you. Furthermore, it does not even mean that he or she must know you prior to the beginning of the mentoring relationship.

However, I strongly suggest that you choose someone with some relevant experience. The relevant experience could be a function of certain companies where he or she has worked or of certain situations that he or she has encountered.

When you enter into a relationship with a mentor, you should expect that he or she has experience mentoring professionals. If you expect to be successful in achieving your stated objectives, this experience is important.

In many ways, coaching, leading, and mentoring are all similar. In fact, most often, the three words are used interchangeably. As a matter of fact, most people believe they could be successful doing any of those three things. While on the surface mentoring might seem easy, let me assure you that this is not the case. Therefore, I strongly recommend that you seek a mentor who has experience in mentoring.

Certainly there are some situations in which an inexperienced mentor may be very helpful. Nonetheless, I suggest that you work with someone with a record of success as a mentor. Remember: Just because someone is successful does not necessarily mean he or she will be effective as a mentor. Also, just because someone is a nice person does not imply he or she will be a successful mentor.

Mentoring is serious business. The mentor and the mentee must always be in pursuit of excellence. Your career is too important for compromise. Always select the most experienced and committed person you can find to be your mentor.

Just as any other profession, it requires substantial training and experience to be an effective mentor. As discussed earlier in this book, mentoring is not coaching. It is not necessary to be a successful mentor in order to be a successful coach. I would surmise that some successful coaches do not understand or value the need for mentoring, just as I suspect that some mentors do not understand or value the need for coaching.

Relationship

You should expect a confidential relationship with your mentor. You must feel sure that what you say will be held in the strictest confidence and privacy. The relationship must welcome open, candid dialogue. The mentor must make you feel safe to approach a professional issue or topic with which you believe he or she will be able to assist.

The relationship must always be maintained on a professional level. You and your mentor should establish and maintain a high degree of comfort with each other, but it should not require or encourage the two of you to become friends. Mentoring is not necessarily the foundation for building a friendship. Mentoring should be an excellent foundation for building success.

Commitment and Passion

At the beginning of this chapter, I discussed honesty, trust, and integrity. Well, once again I want to stress how important these qualities are if you expect to have an effective relationship with your mentor. However, having a relationship built on trust, intellectual honesty, and high integrity is just not enough. You must also have commitment and passion.

Commitment

When establishing a mentoring relationship, it is important to frame the duration. Ideally, it might be wonderful if the relationship endured for a lifetime. However, nothing lasts forever. Scheduling difficulties may arise, conflicts may develop, work functions may change, and needs may change.

Each party should make at least a minimum length of commitment. I suggest a minimum of 180 days. Any time less than six months will most likely produce marginal results. It will take several sessions just to define and reach a clear understanding of your personal career objectives. Since this is the foundation for developing the strategic plan, this discussion should never be rushed. As a consequence, it takes time for the mentor and the mentee to get appropriately aligned.

If a mentor can't commit to at least six months of support for the mentee, you should never initiate the relationship.

Be mindful that you may choose to have a variety of associations with different individuals. I am only referring to a serious mentoring relationship. If the mentor can't allocate the appropriate time, you should move on and keep looking.

After the first three months, either party should have the option to terminate the relationship at any time. However, once again, for the first three months, both parties should be committed to the relationship. This is important because both must make a substantial investment of time and effort to make the mentoring relationship work. Then, after the first three months, either party should not a feel any burden should one choose to sever the relationship for whatever reason.

Passion

Even if a mentor with all the relevant expertise and availability is deeply committed to mentoring you, the relationship will be lacking unless he or she feels a strong passion for working with you. If your mentor does not share your excitement and enthusiasm for pursuing your objectives, he or she could become a hindrance to your success rather than a positive influence.

Therefore, your mentor should not be someone who is merely assigned to you or someone who feels obligated to do it. Your mentor must display a sense of passion for your personal objectives. If you expect your mentor to be fully engaged with you, then he or she should be excited about working with you. Your success will be greatly influenced by the knowledge and level of engagement demonstrated by your mentor.

MENTORING SCHEDULE

TOOLS You should expect to keep in regular contact with your mentor with a combination of phone, e-mail, and in-person sessions, if possible. For a six-month to a year schedule, you should consider your areas of focus and your objective for each meeting. Although your plan should be focused, you may elect to leave the last few sessions available for wrap-up and discussion. Additionally, as your overall objective may change, your plan should accordingly allow for new areas of focus. Meeting at least twice a month for one and a half hours per session should provide a consistent and advantageous program. Figure 4-1 shows the mentoring schedule used at XCEO, Inc.

Session	Date	Venue	Time	Area of Focus	Objective

Figure 4-1. XCEO mentoring schedule

Results

What you ultimately want to receive from your mentor is results. The best-laid plans and best efforts don't really matter if you fail to achieve your goal.

To generate the results you expect from a mentoring relationship, you must develop an appreciation for how your mentor thinks. To do so, this will require a high level of engagement between the two of you.

For your mentor to fully understand your particular needs, you must communicate these needs consistently. You must be clear and concise with your mentor. You and your mentor must both foster interactions on a regular basis in order to establish well-defined, shared expectations. When you and your mentor have shared expectations, there will be little room for ambiguity.

Always be mindful that your mentor, like you, has emotional needs. He or she will seek opportunities to assess your approval of his or her work. Therefore, you should show a genuine interest in your mentor in order to leverage the

> **SEEK THE OPPORTUNITY TO TELL THE TRUTH**
> **FOR EXAMPLE**
>
> I look for opportunities to present truthful information to the people with whom I work. Rather than waiting for a colleague or client to raise a question, I try to anticipate what he or she needs or wants to know. I seek the opportunity to tell these people the truth, even before they pose the question.

effectiveness of your relationship. Never underestimate the power of the mentor's emotional needs. You ignore them at your peril.

To improve the odds of achieving your objectives, engage your mentor thoughtfully. Ask constructive, penetrating questions and then listen intently.

Gaining a sense of your mentor's values and history will help you understand how to establish a successful working relationship. That is the key to getting the results you want.

Now that we know who needs a mentor and what a mentee should expect from a mentor, it's time to focus on what the mentors provide for their protégés. The next five chapters will review five types of mentoring relationships—professional mentor, formal corporate mentor, informal corporate mentor, peer-to-peer mentor, and friend or family mentor. In each chapter, we will highlight some of the substantial differences and advantages associated with that type of mentoring. Each chapter will follow a similar format: begin with a general introduction and then give an overview of the structure, qualifications, methodology, types of services, and typical investment associated with each mentoring program.

Manager's Checklist for Chapter 4

☑ Maintain the highest level of integrity in any mentoring relationship. Show yourself worthy of being trusted. Promote open communication.

☑ Remember: The effectiveness of a mentoring relationship will be influenced by personality match.

☑ Provide a safe, nurturing place for the employees you mentor to broach any professional issues or topics they deem important to their success.

☑ Never compromise the confidentiality of a mentoring relationship.

☑ Be mindful that mentoring should help develop abilities and knowledge, but not necessarily develop a friendship.

☑ You should share the enthusiasm that any employees you mentor feel about pursuing their objectives.

☑ Remember: Results count. The best plans and efforts do not really matter if the mentees fail to achieve their goals.

The Professional Mentor

I t might seem, at first glance, like a natural instinct for an organization to value and develop the skills of the people who are responsible for the success of that organization—but often such is not the case. Ironically, when business slows down and revenues or profits begin to decline, some managers cut back on employee development. At first, this may represent the line of least resistance for cutbacks. However, it is unreasonable to cut back on people development in hopes of producing positive consequences for the shareholders.

Cost certainly will continue to be an important factor in competing or even surviving. However, I strongly believe that the people side of business will continue to demand managers' ever-increasing attention. Managers should invest more money and energy in developing people who have the creative instincts to imagine new products and services and the drive to turn their ideas into money.

Professional mentors can help managers provide every employee in an organization encouragement, support, and opportunities for personal development. It is an important way to build value for all of the company's stakeholders. In addition, these professionals work directly for high-aspiration individuals.

Professional mentoring can be one of the most effective ways of assisting managers and leveraging the productivity of their organizations. Professional mentors enable managers to efficiently maintain a focus on

KEY TERM **Professional mentor** Someone who dedicates his or her skills and experiences to supporting the development of other individuals, generally providing his or her services for a fee.

Professional mentors partner with public and private corporations and with not-for-profit organizations to help them develop their high-aspiration and high-potential employees. Professional mentors are very selective when considering potential protégés.

training and people development during good times as well as bad times.

Using a professional mentor will also provide advantages for the employee. These external mentors are more likely to be totally objective in assessing the individual's performance, potential, and career aspirations. In addition, a professional mentor should bring experiences that are in line with what the mentee needs. Finally, a professional mentor would not feel threatened by the mentee's career objectives.

A recent annual report on the U.S. training market (Bersin & Associates, *2009 Corporate Learning Factbook*) showed that companies cut their training budgets by 11 percent in 2008—the fastest rate decline in 10 years. That statistic, which is not startling in today's economic environment, indicates how much corporations are shifting their reliance on social networking and mentoring.

I believe Jessica Stillman sums it up aptly: "So what is the point for managers … ? The takeaway lies in Bersin's findings on what replaced all this lost formal training: collaboration, knowledge sharing, social networking, coaching, and mentoring. These more informal, lost-cost methods of sharing knowledge within an organization have shown an uptick as employers look for ways to invest in their employees despite the turndown. Perhaps they deserve a look as a way to both productively occupy workers through the downturn and as programs that will help firms emerge stronger when the economy begins to awaken again" ("Training Down, Mentoring Up," *www.bnet.com*, January 27, 2009).

Professional mentoring can be a valuable service for experienced executives as well as new employees. The need for mentoring is not simply gauged by an individual's age or experience.

Professional mentors must have a passion for developing people.

They should demonstrate excitement for the opportunity to support the mentee and be in constant pursuit of his or her success.

The returns on the investment in a professional mentor will usually be directly correlated with the effort the employee devotes to the program. Being mentored is hard work, but a mentoring program will deliver substantial returns on the investment.

For Example

Corinne Wayshak was an experienced entrepreneur when she became president and chief executive officer of a startup company, Confoti, Inc., in Sunnyvale, California, in 2001. However, she decided to seek a professional mentor. Wayshak acknowledges that she went seeking an "executive tune-up" for herself and the company to more effectively deal with the new challenges they would face. According to Wayshak, after a rigorous interview process, she was accepted into a professional mentoring program and paired with an experienced mentor who provided her support and guidance during the next 12 months.

She acknowledges that prior to this relationship she was reluctant to seek help. This was new territory for her. Like many executives, she was independent, self-confident, and perhaps a bit stubborn. She says she elected to try a professional mentor after a dinner meeting with the president of a business unit of Levi Strauss & Co. Wayshak is now an advocate of seeking help in a formal way from a mentor. (Corinne Wayshak, "A Business Case for Formal Mentoring," *Entrepreneurship*, www.entrepreneurship.org, 2008.)

What Is a Professional Mentor?

Professional mentors are individuals who dedicate their skills and experiences to supporting the development of

WHY GO WITH A PRO?
Corinne Wayshak explains several advantages when choosing a professional mentor: "In many respects, the fact that I paid for a mentoring program has allowed me to view mentoring in a new light. The program's value-add is that of a rigorous screening process that would well match me to a mentor. I wouldn't be imposing on this person but rather securing what I was owed under a contract. A fee-based arrangement, moreover, could mitigate the ups and downs inherent to informal mentoring relationships, where building rapport is paramount and results are far from certain."

other career-oriented professionals, generally for a fee. They inspire individuals to perform at the highest levels of their capability to earn opportunities to pursue their long-term career aspirations. Professional mentors are very selective when considering potential protégés.

Professional mentors hold a unique position in the people development industry. There are similar positions, such as executive coaches. Although, as discussed in previous chapters, there are substantial differences between coaching and mentoring, professional mentors and executives coaches compete for the same dollars from individuals and corporations. Professional mentors also compete against other types of mentors who provide their services without charging a fee.

Professional mentors can be considered as an alternative to attending seminars and external development programs offered by academic institutions and professional teaching organizations. Also, similar services may be offered by traditional outplacement service companies and training organizations.

What Is a Professional Mentoring Program?

Let's look at what's involved in setting up a professional mentoring program.

Structure

Professional mentoring programs should be structured to fit the specific needs of the client. Start dates and completion dates are generally well defined. These programs are typically interactive: the process is designed to ensure open dialogue between the mentor and the mentee. The programs should provide an assessment of the mentee's background and his or her career aspirations, and the structure should allow the identified needs to be incorporated into the program.

A professional mentoring program should provide the mentee with informational materials appropriate to his or her specific needs. In particular, if the mentor has published articles or books on topics that are specifically related to those needs, they are likely to be incorporated into the program.

The professional mentor will have access to a variety of training and development exercises and instruments that are generally available, such

PRINCIPLES ANALYSIS

TOOLS

XCEO, Inc., designed the XPL Principles Analysis in order to accurately assess a mentee's aptitude in relation to the 11 extreme personal leadership principles as presented in *Corporate Rise* (Crawford, 2005). Following the advice contained in this book will help mentees develop the skills, behaviors, and attitudes necessary to accelerate their career progress. The purpose of the XPL Principles Analysis is to help them better understand their career performance in terms of these 11 principles. Once mentees have completed the exercise, they receive their score and a personal action for the exercise. Additionally, the analysis provides an output summary and, more important, offers development recommendations for immediately improving their careers (*www.corporaterise.com*).

as personality tests, behavioral tests, and personal skills assessments. These tools will help the mentor and the mentee come to a common understanding of the current situation. The results of these exercises and instruments will enable them to develop appropriate plans and activities.

Many factors will contribute to the mentees' success, including every person around them. The relationships they form during their careers—with senior management, their spouse or significant other, and friends—will inevitably affect their success. Because of the significant role of stakeholders in their careers, it is crucial to understand how they are being assessed by those around them.

The support infrastructure provided by the professional mentor should be comprehensive enough to address all the concerns and needs of the mentee. In other words, the staff and other external resources, such as

STAKEHOLDER SUPPORT ANALYSIS

TOOLS

To help mentees better understand the stakeholders in their careers, XCEO, Inc. offers the Stakeholder Support Analysis (*https://www.xceo.net/analysis/index_p_s_analysis.cfm*). This analysis includes their supervisor, peers, and other managers at all levels. After completing the Stakeholder Support Analysis, the mentees receive their results immediately. The results include their current Stakeholder Support Level, their discernible stakeholder activities and how their stakeholders are supporting them, and finally what XCEO, Inc. believes they should be doing to build better relationships with their stakeholders. (See Figure 5–1)

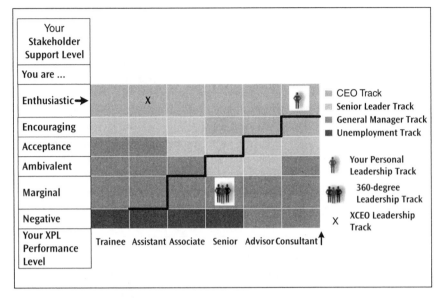

Figure 5-1. Extreme personal leadership analysis and stakeholder support analysis: combined analysis chart

industry experts, should be readily available to the mentee. The structure might include individuals who are skilled in such areas as project management, brand management, resource development, and career counseling. Other types of infrastructure support could include information technology assistance and networking partnerships.

The professional mentor should bring a comprehensive set of tools to the relationship that his or her protégé would not typically have access to. Furthermore, the use of these tools and other resources should obviously be held at the highest level of confidentiality. This is another distinct advantage of working with a professional mentor.

Services

Counseling with the protégé should be the basis for all other services provided by the professional mentor. Generally, the broader array of services offered should include consulting, advising, teaching, listening, and thinking. The consulting process should be an integral part of the basic mentoring agreement. The mentor should be readily available to help the mentee deal with real-time situations as they develop throughout the mentoring relationship.

Advice and consulting services are most likely to be provided to meet specific needs that are surfaced by either party. On the other hand, teaching should be integrated into the professional mentor's program such that it becomes an integral part of everything that he or she does. The mentor must maintain a focus on teaching the protégé things that will help him or her improve the odds of achieving career objectives.

Perhaps the most important part of the relationship will be built around the professional mentor's ability to listen attentively to the needs of the protégé. The mentor must be able to listen and grasp the real meaning of the individual's career aspirations. The mentor must listen for things that are not said as well as things that are said. Of course, the foundation for understanding what has been said and what has not been said is the ability to think about issues and opportunities in a way that is in the best interest of the protégé.

When a protégé defines his or her aspirations, the professional mentor should not accept them at face value. The mentor should challenge the protégé in order to better understand and appreciate his or her passion and commitment. It is important for the mentor to reflect on the intellectual content of the discussion. Listening and thinking, listening and thinking, listening and thinking: this is the foundation for developing a true understanding of the needs of the protégé.

Process

Professional mentoring programs are delivered in various ways. The mentoring can be delivered in the framework of a controlled program. Here, the mentor provides support through regular one-on-one consulting sessions. The mentorng can also be delivered only as needed.

The professional mentor's program should include a comprehensive set of processes to help facilitate an efficient and effective collaborative environment for the protégé. These various processes will be used interchangeably.

In the beginning, the professional mentor will stress the need for in-person meetings with a protégé. These initial meetings are important in establishing confidence, trust, and familiarity. As the relationship develops, the mentor and the protégé may not need to meet in person each time. They may use other communicative processes.

An alternative to in-person meetings, such as WebEx seminars, is used to maintain an in-person type of an environment while minimizing the need for travel. This process can substantially reduce the overall investment necessary to sustain an effective mentoring relationship. Of course, basic telephone conferencing works well between parties who have an established relationship.

The key to building a successful communicative process is the integration of various methods and mediums to enhance the interactions between the mentor and the protégé. Therefore, the professional mentor integrates and interweaves phone calls, in-person meetings, and online Web collaboration.

Networking is a very important part of the communication process. The professional mentor will work to ensure that the protégé has the right opportunities to meet individuals who can substantially impact his or her long-term career aspirations. Networking is one of the more effective ways of introducing individuals.

Networking is important because it provides opportunities for the mentee to be introduced to the right people and gain visibility. However, it is important to be mindful that along with visibility comes exposure. The professional mentor understands the difference between the two. Exposure can be detrimental if the mentee does not perform well—or advantageous if the mentee performs well. The mentor can help the mentee present himself or herself in a way that turns exposure into a positive experience.

Networking can be accomplished in a variety of ways. There are some networking activities where hundreds of individuals are invited to participate, all hoping for the opportunity to meet someone who could have an impact on their careers. In this type of environment, the mentee may have an opportunity to get to know a few important people. Another approach, which most professional mentors prefer, is to introduce a mentee to a few people who can have a profound impact on his or her career. It is always better when the mentor arranges for the mentee to have lunch with someone with influence than when the mentee participates in an activity with 100 people passing out business cards.

In networking, it is obviously better to introduce yourself than to not do so. However, having meaningful dialogue with people you meet is obviously much better than not doing so.

Enlightened mentors understand the difference between "whom you know" and "who knows you." As I suggested in an earlier chapter, whom you know is relatively unimportant. In business, the only thing that counts is who knows you. Many people in business know Bill Gates is, but it is not very helpful to them. However, those individuals Bill Gates knows can most likely benefit from that relationship. Again, whom you know is unimportant. What counts is who knows you.

Duration

A professional mentoring program will likely offer multiple options. For example, XCEO, Inc. offers mentees four options (silver, gold, gold plus, and specialized). Each program has unique characteristics. They vary in duration from three months to two years, in the number of engagements between the mentor and the protégé, and in the length of each engagement. The professional mentor has to assess the needs of the potential protégé and suggest the program that seems most appropriate for most effectively helping him or her achieve the stated career objectives.

Availability

Availability is an important criterion when evaluating potential professional mentors. The mentor must be able to allocate sufficient time to be responsive to the needs of the mentee. A professional mentor is basically on call all the time. He or she should provide the protégé with contact information so that the protégé is able to reach the mentor should help be needed. Of course, professional courtesy and respect are expected from both parties. But the mentee should not hesitate to contact the professional mentor at any time when needed. The mentor is there to serve the mentee.

Cost

Professional mentoring is a fee-based service, unlike traditional mentoring. While professional mentors are likely to be passionate about their work, they are also well compensated for their services. Many of them function as sole proprietorships or work in limited partnerships. However, some professional mentors work in organizations that provide services beyond mentoring.

Professional mentoring fees will vary according to the experience of the mentor, the type of services offered, and the quality of the programs. A simple online professional mentoring program will understandably be substantially less expensive than a one-on-one counseling engagement with a seasoned executive.

Managers should consider mentoring fees as an investment in their employees. Likewise, individuals who hire mentors should consider it an investment in themselves. Usually, there will be a direct positive correlation between the fees and the services rendered.

Professional mentors usually develop their fee structures based on an hourly rate for their services. Some actually charge an hourly fee. These fees can range from $150 to more than $500 per hour.

Other professional mentors have fee structures that are based on longer-term engagements. Their fees will also include the costs associated with their intellectual property—the products, tools, and services used in the mentoring program. Longer-term engagements with these mentors will require investments between $5,000 and $20,000 per individual mentoring relationship; they will likely provide discounts for multiple engagements.

What Are the Qualifications of a Professional Mentor?

There a variety of qualifications to look for when choosing a professional mentor for your organization. Let's review them.

Skills

In our lives we can usually get by with our own experiences, relying only on our own familiar points of view. However, during times of conflict and difficulty, the ability to drop our point of view and see another point of view can be extremely helpful. This takes a unique set of skills.

Philosophy plays an important role in a professional mentoring relationship. Philosophy is an activity, not a body of knowledge. Simply stated, philosophy is the ability to see oneself and others from various points of view. A professional mentor will work with the mentee to help him or her view the strengths and weaknesses of various points of view.

The mentor must demonstrate knowledge and empathy when encouraging consideration of other viewpoints that the mentee may see as untimely or questionable. The professional mentor will help explore a variety of points of views in such a way that the mentee does not feel insecure,

> **Philosophy** Most basic beliefs, concepts, principles, values, and attitudes of a person or group; also the **KEY TERM** study of the basic concepts of truth and reality. In a mentoring environment, philosophy is used to help the mentor and mentee establish an effective working relationship. Philosophy is the basis for establishing shared expectations.

using effective listening skills and subject matter experience, as appropriate.

The professional mentor will use philosophy to show the limitations of some points as a way of teaching and helping the mentee move beyond his or her areas of familiarity to look at things from a different perspective. In other words, the professional mentor will help the protégé look at common things in uncommon ways.

Knowledge

Whatever the source of the knowledge, the professional mentor must demonstrate substance. Whether the insights come from direct experiences or indirect learning, knowledge is the foundation for adding value as a professional mentor. Combined with experience, relevant knowledge is a prerequisite for advising and counseling protégés.

A powerful combination of experiences and knowledge will differentiate professional mentors from many other mentors. Operating experience and knowledge gained from both on-the-job training (practical) and education (theoretical) should offer substantial advantages to the mentee.

Experience

A professional mentor should have experience in his or her area. For example, a professional mentor who focuses on leadership development should have substantial experience in developing leaders. That experience might include leadership positions such as senior executive officer, chief executive officer, or corporate board member. It could also include human

> ### Look Beyond the Clones
>
> **FOR EXAMPLE** Employees with high aspirations and high potential should be less concerned about whether their mentors have significant, similar functional experience. For example, in certain situations a sales executive may be the most appropriate person to mentor an individual who is pursuing a successful career as a salesperson, but a person with substantial mentoring experience may be as effective as, or perhaps even more effective than, an experienced sales executive. The choice of a mentor should be made according to the individual employee and the specifics of his or her situation, rather than any general guidelines.

resources development, career counseling, professional leadership development, and education.

It would be most beneficial if the mentor has experience that is either directly or indirectly related to the protégé's career aspirations. However, it should not be an absolute requirement. In a later chapter, we will discuss the advantages and disadvantages of heterogeneity and homogeneity relative to career advisors. For now let me suggest that professional mentors should be able to provide outstanding services to protégés even though they may have no direct experience in the protégés' field.

Experience is usually defined as direct observation or participation or the knowledge gained through direct observation or participation. While the professional mentor may not have direct experience within the discipline, it is absolutely necessary for him or her to have substantial experience mentoring people in general.

Work

Direct work-related experience is important when selecting a professional mentor. In this regard, I believe practical experience trumps education. A professional mentor who has demonstrated substantial leadership throughout his or her career will offer significant advantages to the protégé. The mentor is likely to relate more effectively and, as a consequence, reduce the time needed for the partnership to be aligned around a common set of objectives. But neither work experience nor education is enough. The professional mentor should have a blend of the two.

Education/Training

A professional mentor should have earned at least a bachelor's degree from an accredited college or university. Having an advanced degree, such as an MA or MBA, would be a plus. In some cases, for certain mentoring situations, the professional mentor with an earned doctorate (e.g., Ph.D., Psy.D., or Ed.D.) could be more helpful. However, experience, knowledge, and a passion for mentoring are typically more important than any set of letters behind the name.

In most cases, I do not believe that a particular academic discipline of study is relevant. A professional mentor who majored in anthropology but has substantial leadership experience may be more effective in mentoring someone in engineering than someone with a B.S. in engineering.

NEVER SETTLE FOR LESS THAN YOU NEED

CAUTION

Education is a great way to increase knowledge. However, while going to college and earning a degree is admirable, and extremely valuable, it is not the only means to gaining knowledge. People who have earned degrees do not have a lock on intellect and passion.

Experience is a valuable learning process that generates knowledge too. Again, while working and gaining experience is important, and most often necessary, it is not the only method for gaining knowledge either. Experience does not obviate the need for education.

Education and experience create valuable synergy for the mentee. When seeking a professional mentor, mentees should expect what they get. They have options and should give preference to those who offer a balance that fits their particular needs. The selection should be governed by the perceived best fit for the mentee and the mentor.

There are various associations that certify professional coaches and professional training organizations. However, there are few associations that certify professional mentors. These professional mentors are generally included in discussions associated with professional coaches. Some of them may be certified as professional coaches. The certification process is helpful in identifying those individuals. Organizations such as Professional Coaches and Mentors Association (*pcmaonline.com*) and International Coach Federation (*www.coachfederation.org*) offer such services.

While training is important, these professional organizations focus more on style and process than providing subject matter expertise. They certainly can be useful in helping the professional mentor improve the overall quality of the programs and services that he or she offers, but they're not necessary. You may want to select a mentor who is certified by these organizations, but the lack of certification should not suggest that a professional mentor is any more or less qualified.

What Do Professional Mentors Expect from Their Protégés?

Protégés need to know what's expected of them in order for the mentoring relationship to prosper.

Commitment

Professional mentors expect their protégés to be committed to the program. The mentee should feel a sense of personal obligation to complete the entire curriculum. Therefore, before engaging with a professional mentor, the protégé should be certain that he or she has the resources and the fortitude to stay the course, even during times of difficulty.

If the organization is sponsoring the individual, then management should have a commitment to the program equal to the commitment of the individual. When entering the engagement, management should understand the financial resources it is investing and the personal time the employee will be expected to devote to the program.

In addition, the mentee must be sincere throughout the process. This requires intellectual honesty. The mentee must be capable and willing to speak truly about his or her feelings, thoughts, and professional aspirations.

A professional mentor expects his or her protégé to be fully engaged in the thought processes relative to achieving his or her goals. It is not acceptable for the mentee to expect the mentor to have all of the answers. The mentor is there to help facilitate the decision-making process. In this regard, each protégé should bring to the mentoring relationship ideas relative to what he or she needs to do in order to achieve career goals. The professional mentor should be the driver of the process. He or she should offer suggestions, provide direction, validate or invalidate (as appropriate) the protégé's assumptions and ideas, and create a stimulating environment that will help him or her in the thought development process. This process will help the protégé ascertain whether he or she has a good understanding of what is required to achieve his or her personal career aspirations.

Pursuit of Excellence

Professional mentors should be interested in partnering only with individuals who are committed to the personal pursuit of excellence. Individuals with high aspirations should understand that anything less than the pursuit of excellence will most likely result in failure to achieve ambitious career goals. It is understandable that very few people will ever attain a sustainable level of excellence. Nonetheless, the pursuit of excellence will usually help people achieve goals far greater than they would achieve if they aimed at something less than excellence. Professional mentors know that marginal performance from marginal people with marginal expectations will usually result in marginal success. They recognize that high-aspiration individuals expect what they get and they normally achieve success.

Availability

Professional mentoring programs require a substantial time commitment. Therefore, the mentee is required to be available according to the schedule that is jointly developed with the professional mentor. The mentee has to allocate appropriate time for the engagement to be effective. In addition, the mentee must be available to meet regularly and discuss issues regarding his or her career plan. Of course, the frequency of these engagements will be determined by the structure of the mentoring partnership.

Occasionally, there will be schedule conflicts. Both parties should work to resolve these conflicts as they arise. With proper planning and scheduling, these conflicts should be minimal.

If the organization or the individual is investing in the professional mentor to deliver services of value, the failure to be readily available for planned and scheduled activities should be viewed as unusual and unacceptable. Therefore, to maximize the effectiveness of the relationship, the interactions need to be regular and substantial.

Professional mentoring should be viewed as a process in which each meeting builds on the prior meetings in an effort to reach specific goals in a timely fashion. If these meetings are interrupted or delayed, it introduces unnecessary slack into the process and can make it less efficient and less effective. Therefore, it is essential that the mentee work diligently to be available for scheduled sessions.

Realism

It is important for the professional mentor to assess whether the prospective protégé's career goals and aspirations seem realistic. The mentor is not responsible for determining the mentee's career objectives. Furthermore, the mentor is not responsible for discouraging the mentee from pursuing his or her goals. However, to be effective, all mentors must effectively balance optimism with the realism.

Professional mentors have the responsibility to help their mentees properly calibrate their expectations. If the mentor and the prospective mentee cannot agree on a common set of objectives, they should not enter into a mentoring relationship. The mentor should not take on a mentee if he or she does not believe in the mentee's career objectives. Likewise, someone in search of mentoring should not engage a professional mentor if he or she is not convinced the mentor can help achieve

SMART

MANAGING

KEEPING IT REAL

Mentors are responsible for helping their mentees develop plans and strategies to realize their dreams. Also, they are responsible for helping their protégés keep their optimism in proper perspective. A critical step in this process is testing the dream's reality. Some fundamental questions are:

- What justifies the mentee to have such lofty dreams?
- Are the dreams aligned with the mentee's capabilities?
- Are the mentee's dreams aligned with industry/company opportunities?
- At times, people are inclined to hold the most favorable view on possible outcomes. Mentors must help their mentees maintain a practical and realistic perspective regarding their career aspirations. Professional mentors do not allow their mentees to wallow in an idealized or romanticized view of their career aspirations.

his or her stated goals. To be successful, the mentor and the mentee must have shared expectations.

Challenges

Just as professional mentors should not accept mentees who have unrealistic expectations, it is equally important that they not accept assignments when they do not believe they can contribute substantial value to the mentees' effort to achieve their long-term career goals.

What may seem challenging to the mentee may not seem so to the mentor. A professional mentor must assess whether or not the challenges are significant enough for the protégé to invest the time and money for the services the mentor can provide.

Even when the protégé insists, a professional mentor has a responsibility to not provide services if he or she perceives them to be inappropriate. Professional mentors and protégés should be selective and engage in partnerships only when achieving the career objectives would be a challenge.

Respect

As we discussed in earlier chapters, confidentiality is the foundation for building and maintaining an effective relationship between the mentor and the mentee. Both should expect the other to respect their relationship. When conflicts arise regarding different points of view, they should discuss their differences openly and candidly.

If a mentee is not pleased with the services that are being provided by the professional mentor, he or she should make it known as soon as possible. Constructive feedback will provide an opportunity for the professional mentor to resolve any problems and make adjustments to improve the quality of services that are expected in the relationship. Likewise, if the professional mentor is doing an outstanding job, the mentee should provide positive feedback.

Professional Mentoring and the Organization

In this chapter we've discussed professional mentoring, a formal program for organizations and individuals. It offers management an alternative to a formal corporate mentoring program, which we'll discuss in the next chapter.

PREPARATION AND ATTITUDE— KEYS TO SUCCESS

Proper preparation and a positive attitude will substantially increase the benefits of a professional mentoring program. When managers fail to provide the appropriate training and stimuli to prepare the program participants, the program is likely to fail. Therefore, management must create an environment that excites participants about the program.

Listed below are three main reasons why professional mentoring and mentoring programs fail to thrive:

- The match of mentor and mentee is poor.
- The mentee is unwilling to be open and candid with the mentor.
- The mentor is incompetent.

Professional mentoring is a form of outsourcing some of the leadership development activities from within an organization. Like other training and education programs, professional mentoring should be viewed as an additive to the company's leadership development programs for high-potential employees. While there are many advantages that professional mentoring offers over more traditional mentoring programs, there are a few disadvantages for management to consider.

When corporations choose professional mentoring in lieu of formal corporate mentoring programs, they introduce a third party into the leadership development process for their high-potential employees. However, this is not unique. When high-potential employees participate in any type of external leadership development program, the corporations are engaging third parties. So, in essence, partnering with professional mentors is similar to partnering with universities or other external development organizations.

Professional mentoring is more expensive than informal corporate mentoring programs, which will also be discussed in a later chapter. However, I suggest that, while it may be perceived as being more expensive, it really is substantially more effective. I recognize that informal corporate mentoring does not get measured on the bottom-line performance of the corporation. Managers must always remember that you get what you pay for.

In summary, professional mentoring relationships should be formal. However, as we will discuss in the next chapter, not all formal mentoring relationships are conducted by professional mentors.

Manager's Checklist for Chapter 5

☑ Make sure your company culture will support a professional mentoring program.

☑ Establish a partnership with a professional mentor to accelerate your employees' personal career development.

☑ Set the example, and make sure you have a personal career plan.

☑ Consider partnering with a professional mentor to accelerate your personal career development.

☑ Determine which employees will respond most effectively to professional mentoring.

☑ Learn how to how to justify the investment necessary to hire a professional mentor.

☑ Determine if your immediate supervisor has a personal career plan, and learn how to have a positive influence.

The Formal Corporate Mentor

I n the previous chapter we discussed professional mentoring as a form of formal mentoring—formal because it has structure, resources are committed to it, and it has a defined process with specific objectives. In this chapter we will discuss another form of formal mentoring, corporate.

Formal corporate mentoring programs are a form of traditional mentorship, the oldest form of mentoring. Traditional mentoring has been used extensively throughout time. It has often been elitist in its selectivity. This is potentially its major disadvantage. In some organizations, senior members of the organization tend to select for participation individuals who are similar to them in personal profile, such as age, ethnic background, and gender.

Formal corporate mentoring Mentoring programs sponsored and structured by the organization. They tend to focus on employees with high potential and high aspirations who have been identified as the future leaders of the organization. **KEY TERM** These individuals are provided development opportunities to prepare them for greater responsibilities and senior leadership positions.

A formal corporate mentoring program is woven into the fabric of the leadership development curriculum. It provides an effective way to transfer knowledge from experienced corporate leaders to the less experienced employees.

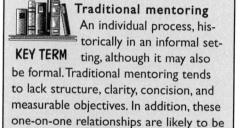

Traditional mentoring An individual process, historically in an informal setting, although it may also be formal. Traditional mentoring tends to lack structure, clarity, concision, and measurable objectives. In addition, these one-on-one relationships are likely to be departmentalized and focused internally. Traditional mentoring is more likely to be initiated by the mentor and associated with informal corporate mentoring. However, other forms of traditional mentoring include peer-to-peer mentoring and friends and family mentoring.

Enlightened organizations are mindful of the implications of actual or even perceived discrimination. It is not only illegal to discriminate in career advancement, but also poor business judgment. All participants in formal corporate mentoring programs should be selected based on the needs of the business.

Formal corporate mentoring programs provide a structured environment for the mentoring process. The relationship in this environment is more likely to be driven by the organization than by the individual employee. The company is more likely to identify which individuals should be mentored. Furthermore, management will most likely determine which individuals should serve as mentors.

There are many advantages of a formal corporate mentoring program for the organization and the individual employee. Formal mentoring programs provide an opportunity for managers to share their experiences about the success of their mentoring engagements. As a result of sharing their experiences, the management team can make improvements that enable the mentoring program to more effectively achieve its objectives. Also, with a formal corporate mentoring program, the process can be made a part of the corporate leadership development program. Furthermore, this program can be effective in transferring knowledge from experienced leaders within the organization to a broader community, resulting in more consistent understanding about the strategic direction and challenges facing the organization.

What Is a Formal Corporate Mentor?

A formal corporate mentor is someone within an organization who serves in a mentoring program sanctioned by the organization and managed by a program coordinator, who facilitates mentor–mentee relationships. Members of the leadership team work with high-potential employees. Usually there is an executive within human resources who is responsible for defining the attributes of the program and tracking performance.

Formal corporate mentoring programs are characterized by their specificity. They are designed around the specific goals and objectives articulated by the mentee. The mentor and mentee are matched based on the perception that the mentor can help accelerate the mentee's career. Both parties understand the value of the program and agree to work within the structure.

The formal agreement is the baseline for the formal corporate mentoring relationship. It provides guidance for the frequency of meetings, time frames, and content. The program is formally structured and measured regularly according to specific goals.

Line managers should be responsible for identifying high-potential employees who should be invited to participate in the mentoring program. As discussed earlier, these individuals should be selected based on their performance and their prospects for career advancement within the organization.

A formal corporate mentoring program should be viewed as an integral part of the overall leadership development program. Employees who are fortunate enough to be invited to participate should view their membership into this program as a clear indication of the company's commitment to their long-term success.

Some of the unique characteristics of a formal corpo-

> **KNOW YOUR NUMBERS** SMART
>
> MANAGING
>
> People development is one of the most significant responsibilities of a manager. Another obvious responsibility of management is producing desired performance results. In my experience, in corporate America the only things that matter to leaders get measured. Things that do not matter do not get measured. Things that do not get measured generally do not get done. Therefore, a formal corporate mentoring program must have targets that are used to determine the success of the program. These targets must be specific and measurable, they must be aggressive, yet attainable, and they must inspire the managers to pursue them with a passion.

rate mentoring program are its exclusivity, the number of participants, and the secrecy. Many corporations do not inform the broader community about their formal corporate mentoring program. The exclusivity is not necessarily intended to convey arrogance. One reason for maintaining its secrecy is to minimize the disappointment felt by employees who are not selected to participate in the program.

Formal corporate mentoring programs usually limit the number of employees who participate. These individuals are chosen through a highly selective process. As a consequence, formal corporate mentoring programs can be disruptive if not managed properly. Managers must find ways to provide other leadership development opportunities for the majority of the employees who do not participate in this selective program.

Management has a responsibility to create an environment that inspires all employees to reach for the highest levels of their capability. When managers fail to do this, they subject the organization to losing shareholder value when employees are not performing up to their abilities.

As discussed earlier, at a minimum, management should expect great performances from all their employees. However, managers who are

TRICKS OF THE TRADE

EMPLOYEES MAKE THE CALL

Managers should look for creative ways to encourage employees to seek opportunities to improve their personal performance.

Management should provide all employees, including those being mentored, with an efficient and effective route to improve personal development.

It is important to allow each employee personal development time. This should not be considered vacation time, sick time, or personal time. It is *personal development* time. Each employee should be encouraged to devote one day each month to improving his or her personal skills or business perspectives. The employee should be responsible for choosing the particular activity and the only person responsible for approving the activity should be his or her immediate supervisor.

These improvement activities should be an integral part of the employee's personal development plan. Further, they should be directly linked to his or her current responsibilities or future career aspirations. The immediate supervisor must approve each activity as appropriate, but is not responsible for the decision.

This program should be available to all employees. While they should be encouraged, participation should be optional. Employees make the call.

moving from good to great, enlightened managers who are performing as leaders, encourage and inspire all employees to perform at the highest levels of their potential.

Corporate mentoring program managers must recognize that the goal is to provide opportunities for all of their employees to fulfill their long-term career aspirations. The existence of a formal corporate mentoring program should not discourage managers or employees from participating in other sponsored mentoring activities.

For a formal corporate mentoring program to succeed, human resources staff and line managers must work together with corporate executives and external partners as necessary or desired. It may seem trite, but it really does take a village to fully develop outstanding leaders.

The human resources staff is responsible for coordinating the formal mentoring activities, ensuring that the program is being implemented equitably across the organization, and monitoring the program for unanticipated or unintended consequences. In addition, the human resources staff has three significant responsibilities.

The human resources staff should be an advocate for the individuals within each unit of the organization and ensure they all have equal access to information regarding the formal corporate mentoring program. The staff should also provide support to line managers in establishing the criteria for selecting employees to participate in the program. Finally, the human resources staff should search for opportunities to partner and share best practices with other organizations within and outside their industries.

What Is a Formal Corporate Mentoring Program?

Let's review the components of a formal corporate mentoring program.

Structure

A formal corporate mentoring program is sanctioned by the leadership of the company. It has a defined process for determining which employees have the opportunity to participate. It also has an organization that provides oversight to ensure that the program is functioning according to expectations. Furthermore, it receives appropriate funding to support the appropriate activities, as defined by the managing committee. The goals and objectives, frequency of engagements, and meeting locations are decided in a contract, or working agreement, prior to the beginning of the program.

The program is reviewed on a scheduled basis to monitor the results. In addition, participants in the program are monitored to assess the progress they are making relative to the corporation's defined objectives. It is vitally important for the management team to allocate sufficient time and energy to provide meaningful constructive feedback to the managing committee.

In each organization, there will be a direct correlation between the number of executives and managers who are participating as mentors in the formal corporate mentoring program and the number of employees being mentored. Given the other responsibilities that each executive and manager will have, there should be guidelines regarding the number of employees that a particular individual should be able to sponsor. This is important for the quality of the mentoring experience.

Corporations should always include some element of professional mentoring in their formal corporate mentoring programs. This will provide a linkage to some of the best practices in mentoring. The professional mentors should be considered to participate in the design of the program, implementation, and delivery of services.

The tools associated with a formal corporate mentoring program are similar to the tools used in a professional mentoring program, although there are some significant differences in how the tools might be deployed.

Both types of mentors are likely to have access to books, articles, and other instruments to be used in support of their protégés. One difference is that the books and other materials used by a professional mentor are more likely to have been written by the mentor. Another difference is that a formal corporate mentor is more likely to have access to a broader range of company-specific tools related to the employees' jobs or the company. This specificity will be helpful in developing the mentees for needs of the company and it may be equally valuable in terms of the industry as well. However, I suggest that managers who are functioning as formal corporate mentors search beyond their corporate boundaries when seeking appropriate mentoring tools and development opportunities. If managers expose their mentees only to company-developed tools and company-sponsored programs, they may limit the growth of their mentees.

Services

The services offered by the formal corporate mentoring program should be similar to those provided by a professional mentor. However, the services are likely to be substantially less. For mentors in a formal corporate program, mentoring is a responsibility added to their job responsibilities. In other words, formal corporate mentoring is mostly a part-time job, even for the most committed and passionate managers serving as mentors.

When they meet with mentees, formal corporate mentors will spend most of the time providing advice and counsel. Because the time available for mentoring is so limited, they are less likely to invest substantial time consulting with their mentees as clients and even less likely to spend a lot of time teaching them.

Most of their activities will center on listening and advising rather than thinking and teaching. Since mentoring is a part-time responsibility, it is understandable that these mentors will not spend as much time thinking about their mentees as they do about their primary responsibilities. Of course, if this is not true, then these formal corporate mentors would be basically functioning as professional mentors.

> **PART MENTOR, PRIMARILY MANAGER** CAUTION
>
> Usually, formal corporate mentoring is not a full-time job. Mentors are either corporate executives or managers with other primary responsibilities. Mentoring is not their specialty. They are usually selected based on their success as leaders and a demonstrated interest in helping others. Formal corporate mentors will devote most of their time with their mentees advising rather than teaching and consulting.

Process

Protégés in a formal corporate program are likely to meet in person with their mentors more frequently than protégés in other formal programs. However, while they may meet in person more frequently, they are likely to meet less frequently overall.

As discussed in the previous paragraphs, since the formal corporate mentoring program is generally an added responsibility, the scheduled meetings are more susceptible to being rescheduled due to higher-priority issues associated with the day-to-day operations of the business. Even in companies most serious about people development, operations will always take priority over mentoring.

Generally, other mentoring engagement activities, such as WebEx seminars and networking, will be less available in a formal corporate networking program. Also, those networking opportunities will be coordinated more likely with other participants, mentors, and protégés in the program. The organization has no vested interest in providing opportunities for its protégés to network with people in other organizations who might want to recruit their highest-potential employees.

TRICKS OF THE TRADE

Low-Risk Exposure

Formal corporate mentors should look for opportunities to introduce their mentees to influential people within their organizations. A mentor should invite a mentee to attend presentations or conferences and introduce the guest to people who may be helpful in his or her career.

A mentor should seek opportunities for his or her mentees to meet with senior-level people by recommending them to serve in "acting roles" during the absence of the executives' regular staff. Another effective way to provide exposure for a mentee is to encourage executives who are perceived as being important to the mentee's future to allow him or her to tag along as an assistant for a short time (e.g., a drive to the airport). When it's only the executive, the mentee, and a driver, the exposure is substantial.

Duration

Employees who participate in a formal corporate mentoring program are likely to participate in other types of mentoring programs, as well. In fact, those who participate in one formal corporate mentoring program are likely to participate in more of the same. For those who do, the relationships that they build during the formal corporate mentoring programs are likely to last throughout their careers.

On the other hand, since most people entering the workplace today will work for five or more companies during their career, these relationships will likely atrophy with time. The employee will usually find employment at another company, within the same or a similar industry, so it is unlikely that the mentor would maintain any connection beyond a friendship with his or her former mentee.

Formal corporate mentoring programs should be simple. To minimize any adverse reactions within the organization, I recommend the same duration for all of the formal corporate mentoring program participants. In fact, I suggest that formal corporate mentoring programs last for one year, that the participants meet at least once each month, and that each meeting last a minimum of one hour.

To benefit from the experience, the protégé should have the opportunity to put into practice some of the recommendations provided by the mentor. Equally important, the mentor should have the opportunity to see some of his or her advice and counsel manifested in results. A formal corporate mentoring program that lasts less than 12 months and meets fewer than 12 times is likely to be unsuccessful.

Setting a standard duration for formal mentoring programs, in addition to making them less difficult to manage, will reduce the friction among units in the organization that would arise if a mentor made different commitments and the mentees had various expectations. Managers should not be burdened with the necessity of explaining, for example, why some individuals are in a six-month program and some are in a nine-month program. Keep it simple and it will be more effective.

Availability

Mentors in a formal corporate program should commit to being readily available to their mentees. The mentees should not feel like they are burdening their mentors when they seek assistance. As discussed in the previous chapter, I believe a professional mentor should be on call all the time. Formal corporate mentors do not need to be on call all the time, but they should be readily available most of the time.

CURT'S EYES ONLY (CEO)

TOOLS
Formal corporate mentors should consider establishing a private e-mail address to facilitate communications with their mentees. As a CEO, I used "Curt's Eyes Only" as a way for my employees to reach me on an intranet site. This e-mail address was not filtered by my administrative staff.

Formal corporate mentors can substantially improve communication with their mentees by providing access to private communication tools such as special voice mail and e-mail addresses. With minimal risk to the mentors, these special communication links will make the relationship more effective and establish a higher level of trust and confidentiality.

Cost

Unlike professional mentoring, corporate formal mentoring is not a fee-based service. However, it is not a free service. Although formal corporate mentors do not directly charge their protégés a fee for services rendered, there is a cost associated with their participation in the program.

Some organizations that encourage, or at least allow, their managers and executives to participate in the corporate program will charge each mentee's department for services rendered. However, a more likely scenario is for each mentor's department to absorb the cost of the mentor's time.

It is more effective when formal corporate mentoring program investments are maintained at a high level within the organization. Typically, these departments will have enough economies of scale and broad responsibilities to accommodate the appropriate checks and balances. They should be able to make better investment trade-offs among leadership development, product development, invested capital, and other types of corporate investments.

Usually, first- and second-line managers will not have flexibility in their budgets to sponsor a successful mentoring program. Formal corporate mentoring is a capital investment program. It should be allocated and managed similar to other corporate investments.

Corporate professional mentoring programs, like professional mentoring programs, have associated costs. When companies implement formal corporate mentoring programs, they must build the infrastructure to support the mentoring process.

On the surface, it may appear to be less expensive to provide mentoring through a formal corporate program rather than outsource some of the services. In some cases, that may be the experience. However, management has to consider all of the costs associated with implementing and maintaining an effective formal corporate mentoring program as an investment. Included in the costs of the program should be the cost of the time that formal corporate mentors dedicate to mentoring that they would typically allocate to their primary job responsibilities.

However, whether employees receive mentoring from professional mentors or corporate mentors, the costs should be viewed as a long-term investment in the future of the company. Likewise, employees who receive the services of formal corporate mentors should view the mentoring as a substantial investment their company is making in them.

There should be a direct linkage between cost of the formal corporate mentors and the value of the services provided. Simply stated, if a formal corporate mentor does not cost the company much, it is highly unlikely that he or she will deliver much value to the mentee.

Managers usually seek the best value for their investments. It is important to remember that paying a little more and receiving outstanding service makes more business sense than paying a little less and receiving only marginal service. Whether a professional mentor or a formal corporate mentor, you will typically get what you pay for. Typically, good things are not cheap and cheap things are not good.

What Are the Qualifications of a Formal Corporate Mentor?

Now let's review the qualifications of a formal corporate mentor.

Skills

Listening is an important skill for all mentors. One major challenge for formal corporate mentors is to listen more and talk less. Rather than using their mentoring sessions as a series of lectures, corporate mentors must listen actively and allow their protégés to learn by engaging in dialogue. Good listening results in good learning.

A mentor needs to understand the issues, concerns, and needs of the protégé, so listening provides an avenue for the mentor to learn how to help the protégé. In addition to listening rather than talking, the formal corporate mentor should look for opportunities to help the mentee. After all, the eyes capture much more than the ears. That is why we often say, "I see," when we mean, "I hear."

The skills of a formal corporate mentor should be similar skills to those of a professional mentor. However, leveraging the skills appropriately can differ. For example, it may be more difficult for a formal corporate mentor to be painfully candid with a mentee than it would for a professional mentor, since the formal corporate mentor has to be more concerned about the implications of his or her candor than the professional mentor.

A professional mentor might candidly tell a protégé that his or her business attire might be acceptable at their company, but it may be a hindrance to long-term career aspirations. The formal corporate mentor will likely be less direct in communicating the same message. Each may have the same objective, but there are different risks associated with their delivery. Managers have a greater obligation to their employees than do consultants.

WHITE SOCKS MIGHT HOLD YOU BACK

FOR EXAMPLE

Looking the part and playing the part are important in business. While substance over style will determine most outcomes in business, how you appear to your clients, colleagues, and supervisors is important. It is naïve not to take your appearance into consideration. In this regard, the formal corporate mentor might feel obligated to inform the mentee if his or her personal attire is offensive and/or inappropriate for the organization.

The professional mentor has no obligation or authority to tell the mentee how to dress appropriately for his or her company. However, the professional mentor is more apt to offer advice about attire if he or she believes it is in the best interest of the mentee. So if, in some industries or companies, white socks are bad for a career, an employee is more likely to get the news from a professional mentor than from a formal corporate mentor.

While formal corporate mentors may have more difficulty with subjects such as workplace attire, they should have substantially less difficulty when discussing on-the-job performance and opportunities for improvement. Obviously, they are much better positioned to provide candid feedback regarding the work performance.

Knowledge

Formal corporate mentors are expected to have relevant knowledge about the company and about specific career opportunities. They should understand how career advancement works within the company—the informal system as well as the formal system. They need to be well-seasoned executives. They need to know, from experience, how the organization works and how to help the mentee effectively leverage the knowledge.

Also, their protégés will expect the formal corporate mentors to understand how things get done within the organization and which important people they need to meet. The expectations for the mentor will be high. So therefore, it is important that the mentor and the mentee set the appropriate level of expectation early during their relationship.

High-aspiration employees participating in formal corporate mentoring understand the importance of power and influence. They recognize the direct linkage between preparation and knowledge. These high-potential employees recognize that knowledge is the foundation for power and that power is a foundation for influence. Further, they know both are essential for advancing within the organization. They are in the formal corporate mentoring program because management has concluded that they have a thirst for knowledge and a passion for learning. Logically, they expect formal corporate mentors to be highly knowledgeable.

Experience

A formal corporate mentor should have experience directly related to the aspirations of the mentee. In the corporate program, it would be more appropriate to match employees with mentors within their functions or work disciplines. Of course, nothing is absolute. However, to more effectively leverage the mentoring relationship, the mentor should be in a position to exercise authority and influence, which is more likely within his or her own unit. A senior sales executive will be more able than an executive from accounting to help a salesperson who aspires to executive levels within the sales channels. Likewise, the chief information officer is more likely than the head of the legal staff to support the career aspirations of a technician in the information systems department. Formal corporate mentors will be more successful when they have the opportunity to be a stronger advocate and more influential for someone within their own unit.

However, it is important that mentors understand the career aspirations of their mentees. Not all high-aspiration and high-potential employees within the sales division aspire to be senior sales executives and not all technicians in the information systems department want to become the CIO. Multi-talented executives are usually more valuable to the organization because the higher you climb, the broader your responsibilities become.

Work

As discussed above, all formal corporate mentors should possess some directly or indirectly related work experience that correlates with the long-term aspirations of their protégés. If not, they should have substantial management or leadership experience. If they have neither of these two requirements, they should not be expected, or allowed, to mentor in the program.

Education/Training

Formal corporate mentors should not be selected based on any specific education requirements. While it is always good to have as much education and training as possible, and it is assumed that most mentors will have at least a bachelor's degree, mentors should be chosen based on other factors relative to the organization, such as job knowledge and

WHO IS THE TEACHER?

Formal corporate mentors are not expected to be smarter or more intellectually capable than their mentees. However, they are expected to have substantially more experience and knowledge. In many organizations, wisdom is valued as much as raw intellectual capacity.

The formal corporate mentoring program matchmaker, typically the human resources staff, should ensure that mentees and mentors are aligned appropriately, based on their interests, intellectual capacities, and personalities. Neither mentors nor mentees should feel obligated to partner if it would be a mismatch. Therefore, mentoring should not begin until the mentor and the mentee agree to the partnership.

personal experience. They do not need to be philosophers, counselors, or experts in mentoring.

Each prospective mentor should receive some basic training regarding mentoring. This should include some basic guidelines regarding their responsibilities and an opportunity to be exposed to some of the tools and other resources available to them.

Also, I advise the sponsoring units to provide training for the employees who are selected to participate in the corporate program. It is important that all parties understand the fundamentals of the program and establish shared expectations.

The training can be delivered in several formats. Some companies may charter their human resources staff to develop and implement an appropriate training curriculum. The employees and prospective mentors may receive the training through self-study programs, online collaboration via WebEx webinars, or university training programs or the human resources staff may simply provide the mentors and mentees with selected books and articles.

A powerful option is to hire a professional mentor to mentor the mentors. This is a traditional teach-the-teacher approach. This option is likely to be less expensive and more comprehensive than a program developed exclusively with the company's internal resources. Highly enlightened corporations are more likely to see the tremendous advantages of maintaining an ongoing partnership with professional mentors.

What Do Formal Corporate Mentors Expect from Their Protégés?

Let's review the answers to this question.

Commitment

Formal corporate mentors expect their protégés to demonstrate a commensurate level of commitment to the program and the organization as the organization and the mentors are demonstrating to them. While there are no binding commitments from either party, the mentors should expect the mentees to apply the valuable experiences and insight gained from the program in such a way that the organization will benefit as well as the individual employees.

All mentees should be required to honor the core values and code of conduct of their organizations. In addition, they should be expected to maintain an open and communicative dialogue with their mentors about their feelings concerning their career expectations and the effectiveness of the mentoring program.

Formal corporate mentors, like all mentors, should expect their mentees to be engaging and thoughtful. However, unlike a professional mentor, the formal corporate mentor should expect the mentee to play more of an active role in the thought development process. In this environment, the mentor is more likely to be responding to the needs and interests of the mentee than probing and driving the development process.

> **WHO'S DOING THE DRIVING?**
>
> **FOR EXAMPLE** The professional mentor encourages dialogue centered on the mentee's career aspirations and how he or she can pursue them. In contrast, the formal corporate mentor works to help the mentee understand how to achieve his or her career aspirations within the company.
>
> In a professional mentor relationship, the mentor will drive the process. In a corporate mentoring relationship, the mentee is likely to be expected to drive the process.

Pursuit of Excellence

The only employees who should be allowed to participate in a formal corporate mentoring program are those who have demonstrated a commitment to excellence. Therefore, the mentors should expect nothing less from any participant. The pursuit of excellence should be a key for entrance.

Availability

As discussed earlier in this chapter, the normal and critical day-to-day business activities of the mentor and the mentee will likely supersede all mentoring program activities. Therefore, the mentor should expect occasional conflicts with a mentee's schedule. However, it is more likely that the mentee will encounter more conflicts with the mentor's schedule.

To maximize the success of the program, the interactions need to be substantial and regular. Therefore, failure to meet planned and scheduled activities should be rare. Mentoring is a process that builds, activity upon activity. When meetings are cancelled, it slows the mentee's development.

Realism

All mentors must help their mentees balance realism and optimism. However, formal corporate mentors have the added responsibility of maintaining a high level of employee morale within the organization while developing several candidates for limited leadership opportunities.

At any point, for example, there is likely only one vice president of engineering. However, an effective leadership development program, which includes a formal corporate mentoring program, will likely be grooming multiple candidates for that position. As a consequence, because of the organizational dynamics, formal corporate mentors must regularly calibrate their mentees' expectations. Again, to be successful, each mentor and his or her mentee must have shared expectations. Mentors should not accept mentees who have unrealistic expectations.

Challenges

A mentor should expect a mentee's projections to be challenging. However, what may seem challenging to the mentee may not be aligned with the needs of the corporation. The mentor has to assess whether the mentee's challenges are important enough to justify his or her time. Just like professional mentors, formal corporate mentors and mentor candidates should partner only when they agree on expectations that will be challenging.

Respect

Confidentiality is the key to establishing an effective mentor-mentee relationship. Confidentiality is fundamental to building respect between the parties. The mentor should give the mentee the same level of respect as the mentor expects to receive.

Most likely, the formal corporate mentor will be a high-level manager or executive within the firm. In this regard, the mentor will command a certain level of respect because of his or her position within the company. However, the mentor should not simply expect respect from the mentee because of his or her title, but instead seek to earn respect through his or her performance as a mentor. Therefore, formal corporate mentors must be careful not to exercise their authority in a mentoring relationship. Instead of *commanding* performance, they must *inspire* performance.

On the other hand, the mentee is less likely to command respect merely because of his or her professional position. Therefore, the mentee must also earn respect through his or her performance on the job and commitment to the mentoring experience.

A mentee engaged in a relationship with a professional mentor can sever that relationship at any time without the risk of retaliation. However, a mentee engaged with a formal corporate mentor will find it more difficult to disengage without some risk.

If a mentee is not pleased with the support from his or her formal corporate mentor, the mentee should make it known to the mentor. If the relationship does not improve, after a reasonable effort of trying, the mentee should constructively disengage as soon as possible.

Setting Up a Formal Corporate Mentoring Program

Implementing a formal corporate mentoring program requires considerable planning. When organizations fail to plan, they risk the success of the formal corporate mentoring program. To minimize the risk of failure, there are three major steps to take before beginning implementation.

First Step: Gain Commitment from the Top

Commitment from the top of the organization is critical, because it means a commitment of appropriate resources and time to build and sustain a successful mentoring program. In this regard, the CEO should be visibly supportive and available to demonstrate the organization's commitment to leadership development. The CEO must make it clear to the senior leadership team that mentoring is going to be an integral part of the corporation's personal development activities.

All the senior executives in the firm should be strongly encouraged to take on the responsibility of mentoring an employee. I am not suggesting that all senior executives should be mentors. Just like professional mentors, formal corporate mentors should be passionate about mentoring. However, I am suggesting that all senior executives who have the ability to mentor effectively be strongly encouraged to participate in the program. Those senior executives who do not have the skills or perhaps the temperament or interest to mentor should be expected to support the program enthusiastically.

For the program to be successful, the CEO has to set the tone at the top. If the CEO is fully engaged in the mentoring program, other officers will be more interested in participating. Again, I do not recommend that the CEO make it mandatory for all senior officers to be mentors, but I do highly recommend that the CEO make it mandatory for all senior officers to be supportive of the program.

Anyone in the organization who has responsibility for managing the work of others—senior executives, middle managers, and first-line supervisors—should be expected to fully support the formal mentoring program. In addition to providing the appropriate resources and demonstrating a commitment to the program, the management team must ensure that the program is inclusive. The program must be open to all employees who meet the requirements for participation.

While mentoring should be open to every employee, it is not necessary to select all of those who are interested. Also, not all potential mentors need to participate at all times.

> **Tone at the top** The connection between personal leadership development activities and support from **KEY TERM** the CEO creates the learning environment for the organization. The "tone at the top" of an organization refers to the atmosphere created in the workplace by the leaders.
>
> The tone, which is set by the CEO, will spread throughout the entire organization and affect all the employees. In general, managers will uphold and follow the lead of the CEO. However, if the organization's leader shows either disregard or disinterest in the organization's personal leadership development activities, managers are likely to do the same. Their attitude is important, because employees will assess management's commitment to the program based on their actions.

Second Step: Define Shared Expectations

The mentors, the mentees, and management must agree on expectations for the formal corporate mentoring program. Managers must identify the potential benefits for the organization. Specifically, how will the program be measured for success? For example, as a result of the mentoring program, should the organization expect a reduction in the attrition rate among its most desirable high-performance employees?

The question of measuring the effects is central to defining expectations. If management fails to define its expectations and, further, fails to gain shared expectations from the participating mentees, the program will likely fail, too. It is more difficult to develop and maintain trust and teamwork in organizations with significant mentoring relationship failures. Organizations that fail to establish trust will fail to succeed.

A mentoring program will not eliminate attrition among the most desirable employees. As a matter of fact, a successful formal corporate mentoring program might actually increase the attrition rate in the short term. As your employees develop their talents and become more valuable to you, they will also become more valuable to other organizations. Therefore, you should expect, as you develop some of your best people, to eventually lose some.

However, in the long term, the organization will attract higher-quality applicants and you will be able to hire more selectively. High-performance companies attract high-performance people. Again, remember the words of Zig Ziglar quoted earlier in this book: "The only thing worse than investing in your people and losing them is not investing in them and keeping them." It is better to develop your people and lose a few of them than to keep them all as they are.

Third Step: Decide Who Will Participate

As discussed earlier, all employees should have the opportunity to participate in a mentoring program, but each should earn that opportunity. So management should define specific criteria for selecting participants.

Since no employee should be required to participate in the program, management should create a perceived set of expectations and rewards for participating. For example, management could decide that employees who are defined through their human resources programs as showing high potential be given highest priority in the formal corporate mentoring program. In addition, management could include employees with unique skills that are in short supply and likely to be in the future.

When employees demonstrate strong leadership skills and consistently achieve their performance objectives, they are more likely to be considered prime candidates for the mentoring program. However, these employees should also express an interest in advancing their careers and a desire for mentoring.

Individual performance is important only when it is part of a winning cause. That is why employees who earn the opportunity for mentoring by their performance must be respected by their peers for their participation.

A corporate mentoring program should bring the best out of the participants. However, the program must be designed so that it inspires support for those who participate. It should not create a politically charged environment. If political concerns outweigh performance, all employees will recognize that talent is secondary to politics. In that environment, all employees will suffer and, as a direct result, the organization will find it difficult to achieve its objectives. Therefore, the opportunity to participate in the formal mentoring program should be offered based on the potential of the individual employee and his or her contributions to the organization.

* * *

In this chapter we've presented the essentials of formal corporate mentoring. Like professional mentoring, as discussed in the previous chapter, formal corporate mentoring is a reserved program. However, it is designed primarily for the needs of the corporation.

Although formal corporate mentoring is an internal program, managers are strongly encouraged to integrate external sources within their leadership development programs, too. The combination of both formal mentoring programs will provide a more comprehensive offering.

The next three chapters are devoted to informal mentoring programs.

Manager's Checklist for Chapter 6

☑ Seek an opportunity to participate in an informal corporate mentoring relationship.

☑ Assess your comfort level knowing that informal mentoring is taking place within your organization without your participation.

☑ See what you can learn from any informal corporate mentoring relationships that currently exist within your organization.

☑ Check your organization's culture to determine if it is capable of tolerating an informal corporate mentoring program.

☑ Assess your organizations preference for informal corporate mentoring verses formal corporate mentoring.

☑ Identify at least three individuals with whom you would be excited to partner in informal mentoring relationships.

The Informal Corporate Mentor

To this point, we have concentrated on formal mentoring programs. As we discussed, these programs have well-defined
processes and structure as their foundation. Here and in the next
two chapters, we will review the more informal types of mentoring relationships.

We have consistently suggested that formal mentoring programs,
such as professional mentoring and formal corporate mentoring, offer
substantial advantages for employees. Informal corporate mentoring
programs provide another source of career support and inspiration for
employees, but informal corporate mentoring programs are riskier and
less likely to produce substantial advantages to the employee.

Informal corporate mentoring programs may be conducted in various settings. These programs are normally unstructured. Because they
are informal and lack structure, both the mentor and the mentee are
likely to lack passion and commitment. Obviously, it is more difficult for
an informal relationship than a formal program to produce good results.

Whether the mentoring program is formal or informal, as we have
discussed, the primary driver for success is the energy and passion that
both parties invest in the relationship. Consequently, managers should
consider informal corporate mentoring programs only as an option when
formal corporate programs are not available.

KEY TERM

Informal corporate mentoring Mentoring relationships that are not sponsored by the organization and lack structure. They develop on the initiative of one or both of the people. The relationships may not necessarily be identified as "mentoring," but this free-form style of mentoring is very traditional. The relationships generally develop naturally. There may be no negotiating of expectations and nothing scheduled. There is no formal mentoring agreement. In fact, these relationships may not even be recognized as informal corporate mentoring programs.

Informal mentoring is a natural component of relationships throughout society, in the workplace and in social, professional, and family activities. In fact, some researchers have concluded that informal corporate mentoring is more effective than formal corporate mentoring programs.

Some research suggests that informal mentors provide higher amounts of several types of career development functions, including coaching, providing challenging assignments, and increasing their protégés exposure and visibility. Informal mentors were more likely to engage in positive psychosocial activities such as counseling, facilitating social interactions, role modeling, and providing friendship. One result of informal mentoring is that protégés are more satisfied with their mentors than protégés with formal mentors.

These differences may be attributed to the underlying differences in the relationship structure. Informal mentoring relationships develop because protégés and mentors readily identify with each other. Mentors may see themselves in the protégé, and the protégé may wish to emulate the mentor's qualities. Finally, in informal mentoring the protégé and mentor are selective about whom they wish to approach for a mentoring relationship, as it can last for years. Informal mentoring is a strong and valuable tool for developing an employee. It occurs in a relationship that is voluntary by both persons. It is friendship first, learning and career advancement second and third.

Again, informal mentoring happens in many environments. While the focus here is on informal corporate mentoring, I recognize that informal mentoring takes place in areas other than the workplace. However, some of these mentoring activities are not related to work or career advancement.

Informal mentoring is manifested through information sharing. It is a relationship between two individuals in which one gains insight, knowledge, wisdom, friendship and assistance from the other. Either party can initiate the mentoring relationship: the mentor to help the protégé or the protégé to seek support from the mentor.

One reason suggested for the above findings is the underlying differences in the structure of the relationships. Informal mentoring arrangements develop because mentees and mentors are attracted to each other. They are not assigned to each other.

What Is an Informal Corporate Mentor?

An informal corporate mentor is someone who helps another person by sharing information, knowledge, wisdom, insights, and/or contacts. Informal corporate mentoring relationships usually do not have a defined structure or associated process. They are initiated and maintained by the mentor and the mentee. The partners choose to work together: they are *self-selected*. They are more likely to be matched by chance. Nobody else is necessarily involved in these relationships. While this type of mentoring is typically not supported by the organization, it may be effective.

> **Self-selected** When two people choose to enter into a mentor–mentee relationship. The process is defined as self-selected because there are no interventions other than the participants.
>
> **KEY TERM**

An informal corporate mentoring program is less likely to have specific targets and a time frame. There is no formal mentoring agreement. In fact, these relationships may not even be recognized as informal corporate mentoring programs. The relationship develops as the needs of the mentee change. Its overall effectiveness is unlikely to ever be evaluated. The primary selection criterion for this type of relationship is likability.

Informal mentoring relationships evolve from voluntary engagements. The relationship may not be sponsored by the organization, but the organization may tolerate it. Unlike a formal corporate mentoring program, this type of program is less likely to be limited by boundaries.

DON'T ALLOW GAPS TO FORM

CAUTION Even when mentoring relationships are self-selected, they can be perceived as being politically motivated and preferential. Managers should encourage mentors and mentees to speak freely about their partnerships. They should seek opportunities to communicate appropriate information to all members of the organization.

If employees do not know what is going on, they will fill that information gap with suspicions, assumptions, and rumors. Managers cannot afford to have employees making up "information." Employees who feel informed also feel empowered to use the information they receive to contribute more to the organization's success.

There is no such thing as communicating too much. If you think you are communicating excessively, very likely you are communicating ineffectively.

Informal corporate mentoring relationships tend to operate "in stealth mode." Furthermore, they are more likely to develop as a result of work dissatisfaction rather than opportunities for career expansion.

SMART

THINKING WITHOUT BOUNDARIES

MANAGING Informal corporate mentors should think and act as though no boundaries exist within their companies. They should not limit their horizons to people they know. Instead, they should be eager to partner with employees in other units within the organization. There are likely talented prospects throughout.

Effective mentoring requires a broad perspective. Therefore, mentors should not permit internal boundaries to obscure their views of the bigger picture.

One of the advantages of an informal mentoring program is that basically everyone has an option to participate. Another characteristic is that few penalties are associated with failure. If an employee is dissatisfied with the mentoring relationship, he or she can try to redefine it or leave it and start another relationship as frequently as deemed necessary with little regard for sanction.

Ironically, one common characteristic of formal corporate mentoring and informal corporate mentoring is exclusivity. While each program is exclusive quite differently, both run the risk of creating animosity within the organization.

As discussed in the previous chapter, in formal corporate programs, employees are selected to participate based on the needs of the organization. Individuals with high aspirations and high potential are more likely to be invited to participate.

On the other hand, in informal corporate programs, employees are more likely to be selected based on personal preferences. A manager or executive will seek opportunities to mentor a particular employee because he or she wants to do so, rather than based on the needs of the organization.

If informal corporate mentoring programs have any sponsorship at all, by definition, it will be informal. They may be acknowledged by small departments or divisions within an organization. Since informal mentoring is unstructured, the participants are not necessarily seeking partnerships with anyone beyond their relationship.

What Is an Informal Corporate Mentoring Program?

Let's review the six aspects of an informal mentoring program.

Structure

Informal corporate mentoring programs have no structure. Mentoring relationships are developed individually. An employee will seek out someone within the organization whom he or she deems appropriate to be a mentor. There is no definition to informal mentoring, other than that all activity should be guided by the core values and basic beliefs and code of conduct of the organization.

Informal corporate mentoring relationships will generally be initiated by high-potential and high-aspiration employees who will take the initiative to identify individuals who they believe could help them in their career development. In some situations, managers and executives will seek out employees to mentor.

Organizations that have formal mentoring programs will likely have informal mentoring programs also. In this environment, the informal program might mimic some of the activities of the formal program and it is then likely to be more structured than an informal program within an organization that has no formal program.

The interactive sessions between the mentor and protégé are likely to be more secretive. The informal environment is more susceptible to favoritism than a structured formal program. In these situations, the partnership is developed mutually without no required obligation from either party. In this regard, informal mentoring activities have few rules and fewer "referees."

The same tools used in professional mentoring and formal corporate mentoring programs are generally available to informal corporate mentoring relationships. However, there is a substantial difference in the way these tools may be deployed. Since these are ad hoc relationships, informal corporate mentors will not use tools such as books and training sessions. They do not have the time or perceive the need for formality.

MINDS, EYES, AND EARS

TOOLS The most important tools in successful informal mentoring are the ears, eyes, and minds. The mentor and the mentee must both listen intently to each other. The better the mentor understands the interest and needs of the mentee, the more effective the advice will be. A mentee needs a great listener with a good mind who can see opportunities to link his or her personal career aspirations with strategic positions within their organization.

Informal programs are more clandestine. That suggests more secrecy and discretion. Because of concerns about the perception of favoritism, a mentor is less likely to make all of the tools at his or her disposal available to a mentee, including corporate resources such as access to information, use of proprietary software, and corporate networking. For example, informal corporate mentoring programs are less likely to offer corporate networking sessions for all the protégés to engage in shared activities on corporate time.

TRICKS OF THE TRADE

PERSONAL THINK TANKS—A GOOD IDEA

Informal corporate mentors should seek venues to showcase their mentees. They should sponsor activities such as personal think tanks and brown bag lunch discussions, which include their mentees and other employees, to broaden their perspectives on business issues.

Encouraging other employees to participate in personal development activities should minimize the potential rifts between those who are being mentored and those who are not. When employees believe they are being treated fairly, they are less likely to be disgruntled when they recognize that some others are being treated differently. Personal think tanks provide everyone an opportunity to be engaged.

Services

The basic service offered in an informal mentoring relationship is advising. Mentees are more likely to seek advice from an informal mentor than teaching and consulting services. Remember: This is volunteer work and it is typically conducted on personal time.

Process

Informal meetings are the basis for informal mentoring. This suggests that mentees and mentors are likely to communicate via e-mail because it is less intrusive. The second most likely form of communication will be by telephone. It is more problematic for the individuals to meet in person because it will become quickly obvious that something special is happening. Informal corporate mentoring has to be managed in such a way that it does not favor employees for anything other than their performance on the job.

Duration

As discussed above, informal mentoring sessions should be infrequent and each engagement should be limited in time. In general, informal mentoring programs last between three and six years. In fact, some will last for a lifetime. In contrast, formal programs will usually last between three months and one year.

Availability

Mentors who participate in informal mentoring relationships are likely to be available as time permits. Therefore, the mentoring takes place as needed. These mentors are on call for their protégés.

This informal mentoring activity should not conflict with the productivity of either the mentee or the mentor unless it has been sanctioned by the appropriate managers of the organization. However, as soon as the organization sanctions the mentoring activity, it starts to develop into a formal mentoring program.

Cost

Informal corporate mentoring programs are like corporate formal corporate mentoring programs in that there are no fees associated with them. However, there are costs associated with informal mentoring. The cost can be measured based on the amount of time that the mentee and mentor are engaged during normal work hours. Since the mentoring is informal, some of the activities may take place outside of the normal work schedule. On the other hand, the mentor and the mentee may find opportunities to collaborate during normal work hours, which would entail a cost for the organization.

What Are the Qualifications of an Informal Corporate Mentor?

Let's review the skills, knowledge, experience, work, and educational training of an informal mentor.

Skills

Informal corporate mentors must be adroit at managing the potential politically charged climate resulting from perceived favoritism. Listening is important, too. Just like the mentors discussed in the two previous chapters, they need to listen more than they talk. Informal corporate mentors need to understand the mentee's issues and concerns. Listening is essential to gaining understanding from the mentee's perspective.

Since they are mentoring part time, it is not necessary for informal corporate mentors to mirror the skills of an experienced formal mentor. Nonetheless, verbal communication skills are paramount. On the other hand, written communications skills—while they may be desired and useful—are not critical to the success of the mentoring relationship. Informal corporate mentors are not likely to be writing many letters and reviews regarding the successes or failures of their mentoring relationships.

It will be more difficult for an informal mentor to be completely candid with a mentee than a formal mentor. In fact, the informal mentor has to be more concerned about the implications of being candid than the formal mentor and the professional mentor.

Informal relationships tend to be more liberal and friendly. As a result, the mentor and the mentee engagements risk deteriorating to a casual level. The comfort in this informal relationship will make them more vulnerable and expose them to greater risk of saying or doing the wrong thing.

Knowledge

Since informal corporate mentoring programs lack structure and formal process, informal mentors are more dependent than other mentors on relevant knowledge about the company and personal career opportunities. They need to know, from experience, how the company functions and how to help their mentees advance their careers.

Experience

Like other mentors, informal corporate mentors should have experiences that are helpful to the mentee. They should be in positions that provide opportunities to leverage their relationships for the benefits of their mentees. Informal corporate mentors should concentrate their efforts within their sphere of influence. Therefore, most informal mentors are advocates for their own organizations.

Basically, informal corporate mentors do not need specific skills to get into mentoring. They only need to be asked by someone who wants to be mentored. Since this mentoring is unstructured, each partnership determines what the mentee needs.

Work

Informal corporate mentors and their mentees will usually be employed by the same organization. To be valuable, the mentors must have relevant work experiences. If they do not, the mentoring relationship will not be successful.

Further, the success of the informal corporate mentorship will be largely determined by the mentor's earlier work relationships. He or she should leverage these work relationships for the mentee's benefit. The type of work experience is less important than the people with whom the experience was gained.

A HEALTHY CONFLICT

FOR EXAMPLE

A professional mentor might honestly tell an overweight mentee that his or her weight, although it might not be mentioned publically by anyone in their organization, may be a hindrance to long-term career aspirations. A formal corporate mentor is less likely to broach the subject at all. However, since informal corporate mentors are hybrids (friends, mentors, volunteers, etc.), they are also likely to avoid the subject or, at best, jokingly suggest it is not a serious concern. When informality breeds friendship, the mentor tends to trend away from conflict with the mentee.

Education/Training

Employees should select informal corporate mentors based on their professional success rather than any specific educational attainment. While education is important, awards and degrees should be viewed as a foundation for a potential mentor's success, rather than a reason for selecting that person. Employees should select informal corporate mentors according to their needs. There are no special training requirements to become an informal corporate mentor.

What Do Informal Corporate Mentors Expect from Their Protégés?

Mentoring is two-way, and mentors have expectations of their protégés. Let's review those here.

Commitment

In an informal corporate mentoring relationship, neither party makes commitment. Both basically accept a best-effort arrangement.

As mentioned earlier in this chapter, the mentors and their mentees should be expected to honor the core values and code of conduct of their organizations.

Mentees of informal corporate mentoring, like all mentees, should be engaging and thoughtful. However, unlike formal mentoring and professional mentoring, in informal corporate mentoring, the mentor should expect the mentee to be the lead in the development process.

CORE VALUES AND CODE OF CONDUCT IN ALL ACTIVITIES

All mentoring activity should be guided by the core values and basic beliefs and code of conduct of the organization. However, this is more important for informal mentoring relationships, because, as mentioned earlier, they tend to operate "in stealth mode." Any activity not out in the open in an organization is more likely to give rise to questions and suspicions.

In fact, if corporate mentoring—informal or formal—is not guided by the organization's core values and basic beliefs and code of conduct, one might wonder about the value of the mentoring.

Pursuit of Excellence

Informal mentors with records of success will be more frequently pursued by employees who want to be mentored. Their demonstrated excellence will attract potential mentees. However, in an informal mentoring environment, where mentors and mentees select their relationships, the organization's high-aspiration and high-performance people will not have an advantage. This is because friendship will likely be as important as performance.

Availability

As discussed earlier, the normal business activities of the mentor and the mentee will supersede all mentoring activities. With informal corporate mentoring, there will always be conflicts with a mentee's schedule. There are no measures of success in an informal mentoring relationship, other than the ways in which the mentees measure it. Therefore, there are few planned and scheduled activities.

Realism

All mentors must help their mentees balance realism and optimism. In this environment, because there are no rules and limited documentation, informal mentors must regularly calibrate their mentees' expectations. Again, to be successful, the mentor and the mentee must have shared expectations. However, mentees should not have high expectations for informal corporate mentoring relationships.

Challenges

Informal mentors should not partner with mentees who have unrealistic expectations. However, the mentee's expectations should be challenging.

Respect

Respect is a major reason why informal corporate mentoring relationships develop. However, confidentiality is the key to establishing and maintaining an effective relationship between mentor and mentee.

*   *   *

In this chapter we have discussed the basics of informal corporate mentoring. Unlike professional mentoring and formal corporate mentoring, informal corporate mentoring is unstructured and it lacks process. It is a relationship based primarily on friendship and respect.

There are no corporate sponsors and these relationships are initiated and maintained solely by the participants. Although informal corporate mentoring is a free-form program, managers are strongly encouraged to integrate other forms of mentoring into their leadership development curriculum.

In the next two chapters we will discuss two other forms of informal mentoring—peer-to-peer and family and friends.

Manager's Checklist for Chapter 7

☑ Have you ever participated in an informal corporate mentoring relationship?

☑ Would you feel comfortable knowing that informal mentoring was taking place within your organization without your participation?

☑ Are you aware of any informal corporate mentoring relationships that currently exist within your organization?

☑ Is your organization's culture capable of tolerating an informal corporate mentoring program?

☑ Do you prefer informal corporate mentoring over formal corporate mentoring?

☑ Can you identify at least three individuals with whom you would be excited to partner in informal mentoring relationships?

The Peer-to-Peer Mentor

Another type of informal mentoring relationship is peer-to-peer mentoring, also known simply as "peer mentoring." It is similar to informal corporate mentoring. The major difference is that peers do the mentoring, not managers. We include in our discussion peer relationships within the employee's department, throughout the organization, and in other organizations.

Peer-to-peer mentoring has grown in popularity, according to Les McKeown, because of a real shortage of classical (older, more experienced) mentors. He suggests four reasons for this shortage of classical mentors:

- **Time constraints.** Managers are too busy to add mentoring to their responsibilities. Managers are more concerned about the perform-ance of their employees and therefore have less time to be concerned about others and do volunteer work.
- **Employee turnover.** Employees change jobs more frequently. Conse-quently, older and wiser mentors are more difficult to find.
- **Demographics.** More companies are younger, usually with younger employees. Many start-up companies do not have senior executives with years of experience.
- **Product cycles.** In many industries, such as high-tech companies, product cycles are short. In addition, with so many new products, services, and technology, older experiences and perspectives seem to be less important.

Peer Individual who is viewed as having an equal standing with another.

KEY TERM Peers typically belong to the same groups or organizations. They are often viewed as having comparable or the same characteristics. Peer groups may be based on simple characteristics such as age, tenure, profession, or status. In business, peer groups are more frequently characterized by their tenure. When new employees join an organization around the same time, they automatically become part of a peer group.

McKeown suggests that, in some situations, peer-to-peer mentoring is used as a low-level coaching program. However, he acknowledges there are circumstances where peer-to-peer mentoring is a genuine mentoring program, concerned with the development of the individual, not just his or her skills or knowledge ("A Peer into Peer to Peer Mentoring," *www.expertmagazine.com/ articles/peermentor.htm*, July 18, 2002).

As we discussed in previous chapters, every employee in every organization will need the help of others to fully achieve his or her long-term career aspirations. Therefore, high-aspiration and high-potential employees must recognize that seeking help is a sign of strength rather than a sign of weakness.

When employees sincerely include others in their personal career development, they substantially improve their chances of being successful. In this regard, peers are some of the more important stakeholders in an employee's personal development plan.

Stakeholder Many factors contribute to the success of one's career, including every single person around him or her. Whether it is company management, spouses, or friends, the

KEY TERM relationships formed during an employee's career will inevitably have a pivotal effect on his or her success. Because of the significant role stakeholders have, it is crucial to understand how they assess the individual.

Personal stakeholders include competitors, family and friends, communities, customers, supervisors and peer groups. Also included are the company general management, senior management, the company CEO, board of directors, and finally, the shareowners. Although employees may not personally know their board of directors or shareowners, understanding the impact these individuals have on their life and career is essential.

While peer-to-peer mentoring can be valuable to employees, it is also valuable to management and the corporation. As we discussed, investing in people is good business. Therefore, when managers encourage and facilitate peer mentoring, their organization is likely to realize substantial benefits along with those gained by the employee.

Peer-to-peer mentoring can be one of the most effective ways for managers to integrate new talent into their organizations. It provides an opportunity to pair experienced employees with inexperienced ones to help the new employees learn faster. This process can be efficient and effective for a short duration.

While peer mentoring can be effective in the short term, it is not a long-term solution for developing people. For obvious reasons, peer mentoring will create conflicts within the organization over time. Most likely, individuals who participate in peer-to-peer mentoring relationships will be competing with each other when seeking opportunities for advancement within the same department or organization.

When senior employees mentor junior colleagues in a peer-to-peer relationship (functional), they are exposed to some of the challenges and responsibilities as managers. In this scenario, they may have the opportunity to help a new employee develop insight into performance expectations and career opportunities. Of course, the perspectives offered by the peer mentor will be biased toward his or her personal experiences within the organization. Therefore, wise managers will only select mentors who have a positive perspective on the organization.

Some researchers have suggested that peer-to-peer mentoring has become important and more common within

> ### CHOOSE WISELY, USE WISELY
>
> Managers should be very careful when selecting employees to serve as peer mentors. These assignments should be positioned as personal career development opportunities for the mentors. Managers should select only those individuals who they believe will represent the interests of the mentee and the interests of the organization.
>
> In addition to providing some basic training for peer mentors, management must be confident that the leaders among the employees will be excited and supportive of the individuals selected to function as peer mentors.
>
> **CAUTION**

organizations because it may offer some unique advantages over traditional mentoring relationships. Further, they believe peer mentoring provides an effective mechanism for sharing job-related knowledge. They believe that peers can provide the same kinds of psychosocial and vocational support as traditional mentors and that peer mentors are uniquely qualified to provide job-related and technical knowledge.

What Is a Peer-to-Peer Mentor?

Basically, peer-to-peer mentoring occurs when individuals with similar levels of responsibilities partner to improve the effectiveness of one or the other. A peer mentoring program is an informal program that is usually initiated by management. While peer mentoring will most frequently be conducted informally, some organizations implement peer mentoring through a formal process.

Traditionally, peer-to-peer mentoring, like other forms of mentoring, happens through one-on-one relationships. While this continues to be the most widely used method of mentoring, things are changing. Peer-to-peer mentoring is also taking place in groups, by telephone, and virtually. Typically, peer mentoring programs are free form. The mentor and the mentee determine how to most effectively work together. Like other informal programs, most peer mentoring has no defined structure or associated processes.

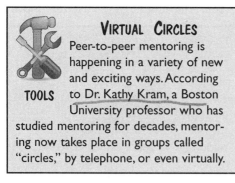

VIRTUAL CIRCLES
Peer-to-peer mentoring is happening in a variety of new and exciting ways. According to Dr. Kathy Kram, a Boston University professor who has studied mentoring for decades, mentoring now takes place in groups called "circles," by telephone, or even virtually.

Managers use peer mentoring as a form of training. When used effectively, it provides an opportunity for new members of the team to learn the basics of the job from someone with experience in that job. The mentor may not be senior in his or her professional skills, but merely have more tenure in the department. In this scenario, the mentor's function is to help the mentee understand how to operate and be effective in a new working environment.

Similar to other informal mentoring relationships, mentors and mentees may seek each other out. Someone with experience may offer to

---

REVERSE MENTORING

In 1999, Jack Welch, then CEO of General Electric, realized that he and his management team knew too little about the Internet. So, he decided to get a young employee who was knowledgeable about the Internet to be his mentor—and he ordered hundreds of top GE executives to do likewise, to find younger employees experienced to mentor them in the ways of the Net.

This form of mentoring, *reverse mentoring*, was around before Welch, but he may have been the first CEO to benefit from it personally. As mentioned earlier, with so many new products, services, and technology, older experience can be less important—and, in many areas, the traditional paradigm of mentoring has been reversed.

---

mentor someone newer because he or she wants to help. Likewise, an employee may seek out an experienced peer in hopes of getting assistance in his or her efforts to integrate into the organization. In either case, this self-selected process can work effectively with or without management's awareness or support.

Like other informal mentoring programs, peer-to-peer mentoring programs will usually lack documented measurable objectives. However, there usually are specific expectations set, either by the mentee or by management. These expectations will typically be the transfer of skills so that the mentee will be able to function as an effective member of the team.

When management assigns an employee responsibility for functioning as a mentor, there should be specific objectives identified in order to measure the success of the mentor's intervention. A simple measure could be how soon the mentee becomes self-sufficient in his or her job responsibilities.

Peer-to-peer mentoring is characterized as an informal relationship and is typically available to all members of the organization. Unlike informal corporate mentoring programs, peer mentoring does not operate in stealth mode. Further, it is usually based on opportunities for improvement and growth rather than resulting from work dissatisfaction. However, it is more likely to be related to work than to career growth.

Since peer-to-peer mentoring partnerships are likely to be widely known across the organization, there is more risk associated with this program than with informal corporate mentoring. Again, peer mentoring is more similar to on-the-job coaching than to personal career advancement. Therefore, if the mentoring is sponsored by the organization, management should expect job performance to improve as a direct result. Even if management is not involved, the primary reason for mentees to seek out peers is to improve their performance in the current job. Therefore, if they fail to achieve this objective, it is likely their jobs will be at risk: they may also fail to be employed.

Again, unlike with other informal mentoring programs, there are penalties associated with failure. If an employee is dissatisfied with the mentoring relationship, he or she cannot simply redefine it or start another relationship. Providing that the assigned or selected mentor is highly recognized or valued by the organization, the mentee runs the risk of being ostracized if he or she fails to respond to the mentor. Therefore, peer-to-peer mentoring is not a risk-free relationship.

Mentees who participate in peer mentoring programs mostly compete against themselves; if they fail to improve on their jobs, they may lose those jobs. However, in addition, they compete against other members of their teams. If they are very successful and master the appropriate skills and knowledge, they are likely to become leaders within the organization over time. In this regard, they are competing against all their colleagues in the department.

SMART MANAGING

TEAMWORK WILL MAKE YOUR DREAM WORK

Developing employees to work effectively as team members is important. One of my colleagues at Lucent Technologies Microelectronics Group expressed it well: "Teamwork is what makes the dream work."

When each person on the team feels gratified and valued, the whole team's performance improves. Not only do the stars shine more brightly, but marginal performers also contribute more. Any employee is much better off working with many talented people than working alone.

Managers who are X-leaders do not think, "I make the team work." Instead, they understand that the team makes them work. Managers must create high-performance environments in which people want to excel.

What Is a Peer-to-Peer Mentoring Program?

Let's look at the elements of peer-to-peer mentoring.

Structure

Informal peer-to-peer mentoring relationships are developed individually. Mentors and mentees seek each other out within the organization based on their individual needs. Like other forms of informal mentoring, there is little definition, other than the need for help or the desire to help. In this regard, informal peer-to-peer mentoring is likely to be initiated by the mentee.

Organizations that have formal peer mentoring programs will have informal ones too. However, these formal programs will have a support structure similar to the structure of other mentoring programs. In these formal peer-to-peer relationships, the partnership is sanctioned, and often established, by management and the mentoring activities have rules and "referees."

There are no specific tools associated with a peer mentoring program. The same tools that are used on the job are most likely to be used to train the mentee. Unless the mentee needs some remedial development, there is no need for the mentor to request or develop any tools or support systems beyond what is required for developing the competencies necessary to be successful on the job.

Services

The usual services offered in a peer-to-peer mentoring relationship are coaching and basic training. However, the mentee is likely to seek some personal career advice from the peer as the relationship develops. Remember: from the mentor's perspective, this is volunteer work—he or she is doing it in expectation that the mentee will become a valued partner at some time. However, the mentor also recognizes that the mentee will possibly become a competitor.

Process

Peer mentors and mentees use the job work flow as their guide for developing their working relationship. Typically, early in the relationship they are likely to meet more frequently to establish the routine. During this

---

MAKING THE SALE

FOR EXAMPLE

Individuals who work as outside salespeople understand the basic rules of engagement when calling on customers. There is a defined sales process. The experienced salesperson, functioning as a mentor, may invite a mentee along on a sales call.

The mentor expects the mentee to watch and learn the sales process. In other words, the mentor is putting on a sales clinic for the mentee. The mentee is expected to observe and to participate only when the mentor or the customer invites him or her into the conversation.

The mentee will earn the opportunity to actively participate in sales calls when he or she becomes more knowledgeable and comfortable with the process. Then the mentor will allow the mentee to take the lead on the sales call and will intervene only when there is an opportunity or the need to substantiate and support the mentee's efforts. When the mentee consistently demonstrates the process successfully, the mentor's job is done.

---

time, the mentee may shadow the mentor during customer visits, as an example, to see the experienced mentor in action.

Frequent communication is important in a peer-to-peer relationship. In this environment, the mentor is a teacher. The mentor is providing more direction during the early stage of the relationship. Then, as a routine becomes established, the mentor is likely to be less involved on a day-to-day basis and to shift roles from demonstrator to inspector.

Duration

Peer-to-peer mentoring relationships should be short in duration. They are intended to help launch someone into a certain environment, not to be sustainable over the long term. In a business environment, a peer-to-peer mentoring relationship typically lasts no longer than six months and a relationship may last as little as one week.

Availability

Unlike other informal mentoring relationships, where mentors are usually available as time permits, peer mentors who have been assigned by management should be readily available to their mentees as needed.

The availability of mentors who are participating in a peer-to-peer mentoring relationship as volunteers should be similar to that of mentors in other informal relationships. That is, as time permits. To these mentors, this is part-time work and therefore of secondary importance.

Cost

Management-initiated peer mentoring programs, like other corporate mentoring programs, have no direct fees. However, there are costs associated with this type of program, too. The cost should be calculated based on the amount of time that the mentor is engaged with the mentee and not able to do his or her job. The cost of this lost opportunity should be included as part of the department's training budget.

What Are the Qualifications of a Peer Mentor?

Let's look at the qualifications of a peer mentor.

Skills

Peer mentors may require some additional skills beyond those necessary to be successful in their jobs. To be successful as mentors, these individuals should possess some skills similar to educators. They must be effective communicators and be capable of providing clear and concise directions. These mentors must demonstrate a sense of caring and empathy for their mentees. They should also be good listeners.

Knowledge/Experience

Peer mentors should focus their knowledge and activities within their profession. Further, these mentors should be engaged mostly with employees within their own organizations. At times, employees should also seek peer mentors from outside their departments and, when appropriate, from outside their organizations.

Like other informal mentors, peer mentors should have experiences that are helpful to the mentee. However, more importantly, they should have skills that are specific to the needs of the mentee.

Work/Education

To be valuable, peer mentors must have relevant work experiences. If they do not, the mentee will not achieve his or her objectives.

As discussed at the beginning of this chapter, our focus on peer-to-peer mentoring suggests that mentors and their mentees will usually be employed by the same organization. In this regard, successful on-the-job experience is more important to a peer-to-peer mentor than education. The specific work and associated training should be the foundation for serving as a peer mentor. Therefore, these individuals should be selected based on their success rather than their formal education.

Commitment

As in other informal mentoring programs, individuals who participate in peer-to-peer mentoring on a self-selected basis have a minimum commitment to each other. Usually, this is a best-effort arrangement—no guarantee of results, no definition of "failure," and no negative consequences.

On the other hand, if the peer-to-peer mentoring program is sponsored by management, there is substantial commitment on both sides. The mentor has a commitment to management to help the mentee become knowledgeable as soon as possible and the mentee has a personal commitment to become knowledgeable as soon as possible.

Should the mentor fail to transfer knowledge to the mentee, he or she may not have an opportunity to participate in future peer-to-peer relationships. However, should the mentee fail to grasp the knowledge provided by the mentee, he or she may no longer have the opportunity to be employed by the company. In this regard, best-effort is unacceptable without results.

Profession/Industry

Peer mentoring programs can be found in all professions and industries. They are likely to be as prevalent in publicly traded companies as in nonprofit organizations. While larger organizations may sponsor formal peer mentoring programs, the preponderance of them will be informal peer-to-peer mentoring relationships.

*   *   *

In this chapter, we discussed both informal and formal peer-to-peer mentoring programs. In addition, we highlighted some of the advantages and disadvantages of these relationships for the mentor and the mentee. There are also substantial benefits to be gained by the organization. When management elects not to implement formal peer mentoring, these relationships are likely to develop on their own. While formal programs may be more effective, it is better to have informal peer mentoring than none at all.

In the next chapter we will discuss the simplest form of informal mentoring—friends and family members.

Manager's Checklist for Chapter 8

☑ Make sure there is an adequate supply of qualified mentors in your organization.

☑ Check your organization for existing informal peer-to-peer mentoring relationships.

☑ Make sure you have adequately trained employees within your organization to serve as peer mentors.

☑ Determine where peer-to-peer mentoring would be most helpful in your organization.

☑ Develop a plan to use peer-to-peer mentoring as an effective knowledge transfer program.

☑ Define your top three concerns regarding peer-to-peer mentoring.

☑ Decide what additional information you need to determine the next step toward implementing peer-to-peer mentoring in your organization.

The Friend or Family Mentor

I n this chapter, we will focus on family members and friends, the last and simplest type of informal mentoring to be reviewed in this book. So far, we have discussed professional mentors, formal and informal corporate mentors, and peer-to-peer mentors. A common theme among these mentors is that each of them is expected to be impartial in the mentoring relationship. In this chapter, we will discuss how impartiality among friends and family members can play a significant role in mentoring.

In general, friends and family members can be mentors. However, it is important that we distinguish between mentoring and providing advice and opinions. While advice can be valuable, we must remember that it is only one of several elements in effective mentoring programs.

Family members and close friends are certainly in a position to provide advice to employees. However, neither

KNOW HOW TO BE INVOLVED

SMART

MANAGING

Management is not involved in friends-and-family mentoring, except in the case of family-run businesses. The mentoring activities will all take place outside the mentee's workplace.

Managers should not seek to get involved in friends-and-family mentoring relationships. However, they do have a vested interest. Therefore, smart managers will always be involved with all employees regarding their personal career aspirations and related personal development plans.

CAUTION

DO NOT CONFUSE ADVICE AND OPINIONS WITH KNOWLEDGE

Friend and family mentors are readily available to provide advice. Of course, advice is simply an opinion about what they believe you could or should do or not do in a given situation. They may offer it freely or provide it only when asked.

They are also willing to offer personal opinions. However, opinions are beliefs that may or may not be backed up with data and cannot be proved with evidence. An opinion is neither right nor wrong. It is merely subjective and may be the result of an emotion or an interpretation of facts.

friends nor family members will provide consistent counseling in a structured environment. Furthermore, friends and family members have a different bias in their relationships with employees than do the mentors discussed in previous chapters.

When an employee has a friend or family member as a mentor, it is similar to having a social network of counselors. While the mentor's intentions are likely to be laudable, he or she is less likely to be in a position to add substantial value to the mentee.

However, a mentor who is a friend or a family member can be valuable to an employee by providing an additional level of support and perspectives that colleagues may not be able to offer. After all, friends and family see the employee in a different light.

Also, friends and family members provide a base of support and comfort beyond what other types of mentors can provide. They are likely to be more sympathetic and sensitive to the personal needs of the employee.

Therefore, family members and friends should not be viewed as being any more or less competent than other mentors. However, it is important that we highlight some of the reasons having a friend or a family member as a mentor may not be in the best interest of the employee, relative to his or her performance on the job and/or career acceleration.

Friends and family mentoring is a traditional form of mentoring that is more aligned with social mentoring. Family members will usually feel obligated to provide counsel and support to other members of their family. In fact, they are likely to provide advice and counsel regardless of whether the employee feels a need for it.

Friends, on the other hand, may not necessarily feel obligated to provide mentoring, but will frequently find themselves engaged in situations where it is convenient and/or it seems appropriate to provide counseling. As a matter of fact, it is highly probable that a friend may be asked for advice as frequently as he or she may offer to provide advice to a friend.

> **KEY TERM**
>
> **Social mentoring** Mentoring that values and emphasizes the importance of enhancing self-esteem, bolstering self-confidence, strengthening identity, and promoting a positive sense of well-being. Also known as *psychosocial mentoring*.
>
> Social mentoring relationships tend to be more informal, open-ended, and less directive than other mentoring relationships. Social mentoring is less likely to be dominated by concerns regarding prescribed outcomes and measurable targets.

In a social setting, having a friend or a family member as a mentor could be helpful. However, unless they have substantial experience relative to the needs of the employee, family members and friends should never be considered as a surrogate for a professional mentoring relationship.

What Is a Friend or Family Mentor?

A friend or family mentoring relationship is informal. This type of mentoring will rarely be conducted on a formal basis. In fact, people may be engaged in some form of friend or family mentoring before they recognize it as mentoring. In some cases, they may never recognize it as mentoring. Some things are just family and some things are just friendship.

Unlike other informal mentoring relationships, an employee in need of help does not need to seek out a friend and a family member to serve as a mentor. They already have an ongoing relationship. In this regard, either person may initiate the intervention, although it is more likely to be initiated by the employee who is seeking help.

The friend or family mentor may recognize that the employee needs help and offer some advice and counsel. Likewise, the employee may recognize that the friend or family mentor is in a position to help him or her in the pursuit of long-term career aspirations.

Since the parties already have a personal relationship, each party might feel confident approaching the other, with little or no fear of a negative reaction. That mutual confidence is a strong foundation for building their mentoring relationship. However, just because the foundation is strong does not suggest that they should build on it. Employees who are seeking help should consider other mentoring options, such as professional mentoring, rather than assume that friends and family members can be appropriate mentors.

Mentoring relationships with friends or family members could jeopardize the personal relationships over time. Therefore, both parties should carefully consider the serious implications before entering into a mentoring relationship. Unfortunately, mentoring relationships with friends or family members do not have any start and stop date. They develop informally over time. In fact, as mentioned earlier, individuals may not be cognizant of the fact that they are engaged in a mentoring relationship.

A friend or a family member who is mentoring must be capable of maintaining objectivity while being emotionally involved with his or her protégé. Their personal relationship should not distort the value of the advice and counsel.

The mentor must recognize the need to occasionally risk hurting his or her protégé by providing candid feedback and at times disagreeing. This recognition and acceptance of the need to hurt when necessary to do good will demonstrate the mentor's commitment to helping the protégé succeed. A mentor must realize and acknowledge that sometimes love hurts.

SMART

MANAGING

Inflicting Pain

Effective mentoring must be based on truth and reality. Therefore, mentors should seek opportunities to be forthright with their protégés at all times. As a consequence, mentors may be required to be brutally honest regarding their protégés' performance, attitude, or career aspirations.

Because of their emotional connection, friends and family members may be reluctant or unwilling to inflict pain on their protégés. Sometimes the truth hurts. Sometimes reality checks can seem harsh. However, while the message may be difficult to deliver, it is better for the protégé if the mentor tells the truth or provides the reality check now than if the protégé finds out the hard way later, when it may be too late.

What Is a Friend or Family Mentoring Program?

The relationship that exists between friends and family mentors is not programmatic. This relationship is personal; therefore, there is no structure or predefined process nor are special tools needed.

PERSONAL THINK TANK

TRICKS OF THE TRADE

Friends and family members who are mentoring should consider establishing a "personal think tank" for their mentees. This semiformal structure will allow the mentors to formalize their relationships with their mentees.

A personal think tank is a group of individuals organized to serve as a center of focus for a specific endeavor. In reality, like many political think tanks, a personal think tank functions to support an agenda—in this case, the agenda of the mentee. When friends and family members are engaged, they have a tremendous opportunity to organize and leverage their thoughts to more effectively support the person they are mentoring.

Duration

Friend and family mentoring relationships can last longer than any other form of mentoring relationship. Family mentoring relationships are impervious to time. In other words, needed or not, family mentoring will last a lifetime. On the other hand, friend mentoring will always be at risk of dissolution. The mentoring relationship will last only as long as the friendship. In fact, it may end sooner if the friends realize that it is jeopardizing their friendship.

Availability

Unlike other informal mentors, family members are always available. While friends may not always be available, the employee will not hesitate to reach out to them. The best friends place no limitations on their availability when they are needed: "a friend in need is a friend indeed."

Cost

There are no professional fees associated with mentoring by friends or family members. However, if the mentee fails to follow the mentor's advice, there may be a price to pay. If friends believe their advice is not valued, it could jeopardize the relationship. Likewise, if an individual fails

GO FREE OR GO PRO?

CAUTION Friends and family mentors will most likely provide their advice and opinions without charge. (There may, however, be obligations or expectations, expressed or implied.) Other mentors, such as professional mentors, are likely to provide their services only in exchange for fees. Remember: just because what friends and family members offer is free, that does not mean it's good.

to follow the advice of the family member, he or she may be excluded from the family trust. In most cases, these outcomes are not likely.

What Are the Qualifications of a Friend or Family Mentor?

Let's review the qualifications of the friend or family mentor.

Skills

Unless the friend or family member has specific skills related to the needs of the mentee, the best skill they may have is the ability to listen. Employees are more likely to talk openly with their friends and family than with their co-workers.

Knowledge/Experience

Friends and family members who are mentoring do not need to be knowledgeable about the employee's career aspirations or have substantial experience in the employee's line of work to justify their intervention. They feel a sense of entitlement because of their relationship. Nonetheless, like other informal mentors, friends and family members should have experiences specific to the needs of the employee they are mentoring.

Work/Education

There are no specific work experiences or education requirements necessary to qualify a friend or a family member as a mentor. These mentors use their personal relationships, rather than education and work experience, to help guide their mentees regarding personal career opportunities. However, mentors who have work experience and/or education directly related to the mentee's long-term personal career aspirations are likely to be more valuable.

Commitment

Friends and family members have stronger commitments as mentors than any other types of mentors. These relationships are not based on the same performance criteria and expectations. Friends and family members are committed to the employee regardless of his or her success or job performance. They are friends or family members first and mentors second. They are not managers and they are not supervisors.

Profession/Industry

Friends and family members do not base their mentoring interventions on professional or industry associations. Whether they have specific experience relative to the employee's needs, they will engage with him or her when they feel it is appropriate to do so.

Mentoring by friends and family members is one of the most sincere forms of mentoring—and one of the oldest forms of mentoring relationships. Because of its tenure, it has obviously been successful.

* * *

In this chapter, our discussion has centered on some of the concerns associated with mentoring by friends and family members. However, in summary, it is important to note that this traditional type of mentoring is the basic foundation that all other mentoring programs are built on.

It is important to recognize that an employee who is being mentored by friends and/or family members should consider other forms of mentoring. An effective personal career development plan should incorporate as many resources as are available to the employee.

Manager's Checklist for Chapter 9

☑ Anticipate the impact on your employee relationship, when you discover that a friend or family member mentor has intervened on his or her behalf.

☑ Reassess any experiences you may have gained while involved in a friend or family mentoring relationship.

☑ Anticipate how you would respond to an opportunity, or agree to a request, to intervene as a mentor with a friend or a family member.

☑ Assess your organization to determine whether friend and family mentoring relationships are more likely or less likely to be as effective as other types of mentoring programs.

☑ Encourage your employees to consider friend and family mentoring relationships as part of their personal career development planning process.

Chapter 10

The Mentee

Historically, mentors have been older, wiser, and more experienced than their mentees. In fact, many have compared the mentor–mentee relationship as a kind of parent-child relationship. While that may have been true in prior years, it is not necessarily true today.

Because of the broad participation and wide acceptance of mentoring, today's mentees are much more eclectic. In fact, it is likely that today's mentees are more educated and more knowledgeable than some of their mentors. Therefore, it would be erroneous to opine that all mentees are junior members of the partnerships.

In effective mentoring relationships, the mentee and the mentor share responsibility for making the relationship work. However, the mentee must recognize that he or she will most likely have more to lose if the relationship fails.

The mentee should take opportunities to demonstrate leadership.

Confidence

Managers must be smart enough to know that they cannot achieve great performances by themselves. To perform with exceptional success, they must rely on subordinates, to whom they delegate responsibility, authority, and accountability. The fact is, management does not have, and never will have, enough time and information to make all the decisions needed by the company. In this regard, management must work

ANYONE CAN LEAD

No one can lead without the ability to cause change in the lives of others. That ability can come in the form of authority. However, it also can come in the form of leadership. In other words, even if an individual does not have direct authority to make change, he or she still can cause change by using leadership skills. In my view, leadership is an opportunity that can be earned (Curtis J. Crawford, *Compliance & Conviction: The Evolution of Enlightened Corporate Governance*, XCEO, Inc., 2007).

diligently to build an inclusive relationship with their employees. They must find opportunities to ensure that high-aspiration and high-potential employees are effectively mentored.

High-aspiration individuals should not be embarrassed about their desires to earn a leadership position within their organizations. These inspired employees should be excited about their work and their prospects for advancement and eager to produce greater returns for their investors than those who are merely putting in their hours in exchange for a paycheck.

Understand Career Velocity

It is important for the mentee to understand and manage career velocity. Most employees misunderstand this phenomenon. Some managers understand the concept of career velocity, but many underestimate the substantial impact.

How *fast* employees advance in their careers will most often determine how *far* they advance in their careers. In general, the faster employees move, the farther they move. However, it will take much more than speed. Career advancement is more a function of velocity than speed. Speed is important. However, velocity is critical. Despite their similarities, *speed* and *velocity* have distinctly different meanings.

Speed A measure of how fast an object is moving, the rate at which an object **KEY TERMS** covers distance, usually expressed as distance traveled per unit of time.

Velocity A measure of how fast an object is moving in a given direction, the rate at which an object changes position. In short, velocity is speed with a direction.

Covering a relatively large distance in a short time is important to personal career advancement. However, speed is not everything. Without a sense of direction, speed is only movement—not necessarily toward a career objective. An employee may be going fast, but slightly off track. An employee may be changing jobs every two years, but not moving closer to his or her long-term career objectives.

> **KEEP DEVELOPING**
> During my 15 years at IBM, I held at least 12 positions, several of them lateral moves, not promotions. Each job was intended to further my development.
> During their careers, employees will be assigned to a variety of positions. All these jobs will be temporary. Never make the mistake of thinking that any assignment is permanent! Think of them as steps in your development. Keep developing!

Career progression is more than just moving rapidly, more than just speed. It requires movement in a direction, velocity. An employee who changes position within an organization must be moving toward his or her ultimate career objective.

Earn the Opportunity for Mentoring

Employees with high aspirations and high potential must earn the opportunity for the organization to invest in their future. To do this, they must be willing to invest time and education, make sacrifices, and compete hard. The employees who will be helped most by a mentoring program are those who are willing to work exceptionally hard during their long journeys toward their personal career aspirations.

If employees dream big and sincerely want to advance

> **GET WHAT YOU EXPECT**
> Remember: as an employee, you should always expect to be treated *fairly*. However, you should never expect to be treated *equally*. How you are treated should be influenced by your behavior, attitude, and performance. If you have high aspirations and high potential, don't expect others to help you develop and advance. You must earn the opportunity for the organization to invest in your future. When you set high expectations for yourself, others will set them even higher. You must earn the opportunity to get what you expect.

their careers, mentoring will help them earn the opportunity to do great things within their organizations. Following the advice of a successful mentor will help an employee develop the skills, behaviors, and attitudes necessary to accelerate to the top of the organization.

Individuals with high potential should have high aspirations and very positive attitudes about their futures. They should be highly motivated and well prepared. They should focus on creating opportunities rather than waiting for a big break. They must strive to do exceptional things that inspire creativity and ever-higher levels of performance. They must be responsible and accountable. They must have high expectations of themselves and their organizations.

One of the early steps for high-aspiration employees in leveraging their talents is to take a good look at things they think they might be good at doing so they can discover areas in which they excel. They should not wait for other people to make the effort—without a strong mentor, it may never happen. Further, employees should not wait for their organizations to find ways to leverage their talents. Unfortunately, many managers will not bother either.

High-aspiration employees should take charge and develop their own way to the top. Of course, making their way to the top will require a high degree of confidence and a willingness to learn, grow as a person, and contribute to the success of their organizations each and every day. All high-aspiration employees must remember that the reward for doing good work always is more good work to do!

SMART MANAGING

LEARN TO LOVE THE GAME

In their pursuit of excellence, high-aspiration employees must liken their long-term personal career plans to playing a football game with mobile goal posts. They deliver outstanding results by grinding them out one yard at a time. As they proceed downfield, they are occasionally cheered and acknowledged by the crowd, recognizing their progress. But they know the game is far from being over. In fact, they expect it to last a lifetime.

As soon as these leaders approach excellence, someone moves the goal posts. Therefore, rather than searching for victories, high-aspiration individuals must learn to measure their success by the progress they make. In other words, they must learn to enjoy the journey because it never ends.

Don't Wait for the Call—Work for It

As I mentioned earlier, mentees should start demonstrating the attributes that they need or desire to master. It is never a good idea to wait for leadership to be granted. Instead, employees must seek out opportunities to demonstrate whatever leadership power they already possess. In order to advance their careers, they should be playing the part.

> ### WAITING IN LINE
>
> I remember receiving some sage advice from a colleague when I moved from Illinois to Connecticut. He said, "When you arrive at a four-way stop sign, the first one that looks ... loses. Looking is a sign of weakness." An interesting perspective to make his point. Fortunately, I did not follow this advice literally. But I must admit that even today I think of him occasionally when I find myself waiting at a clogged four-way stop.
>
> The message in this story is that employees must use the power of their knowledge, experiences, and skills to influence the directions taken by their organizations. They should not wait to be granted the authority to influence outcomes. Instead, they should leverage their knowledge, insight, experience, and passion to their benefit. They are unlikely to advance far by waiting.

As discussed in an earlier chapter, sustainable personal career advancement without teamwork is a myth, and so is teamwork without personal leadership. It is extraordinarily difficult for a mentee to achieve substantial career advancement without teamwork. Mentees must recognize that their success is highly dependent on the achievements of others, so they should work to partner with the best people available in their organizations.

Selecting the right mentor is a major step. Successful mentors will provide substantial advantages to employees in their pursuit of excellence. They help the mentees align their expectations and ambitions, so they are not blinded by their aspirations. As a result, mentees should not find themselves trapped while trying to balance between their personal career goals and the organization's goals. However, mentees should not expect their mentors to have all the answers to all the questions.

Perform to the Best of Your Abilities

The urge to develop one's own talent as an employee might seem like a natural instinct. However, very often this is not true. Nonetheless, any employee who is serious about his or her career objectives must take advantage of all opportunities to maximize the development of his or her skills. Employees cannot and will not succeed in their careers unless they significantly outperform their colleagues.

High-aspiration employees must be more passionate about their jobs and work harder and smarter than others in the group. And they must consistently deliver outstanding results. Outstanding performers are the ones who should be selected first to participate in a mentoring program. Remember: mentoring is a privilege and it should go to those who perform best, have the most positive attitude, and have the greatest potential.

The effort that mentees put into their own personal development will be especially important to them during times of great economic difficulties. When organizations experience financial challenges, high-performance employees will usually be at substantially less risk than others.

Typically, in a business slowdown, the first employees to be laid off are usually those with fewer skills. They are most likely to be the least motivated, the worst performers, and consequently the lowest paid among their peers. Obviously, an employee who is not highly motivated and is comfortable being an average performer is unlikely to advance very far in the company.

On the other hand, those individuals who are highly trained and better educated and have the full support of a mentor are more likely to be honored with broader responsibilities. This provides an opportunity for them to perform impressively, which will ultimately lead to promotions and further career advancement.

Know Your Environment

Mentees must assess their work environment. They must determine whether the organization truly values people development. If a mentee has high aspirations to develop as a leader, but the organization does not value personal leadership, his or her aspirations for success will be thwarted over and over.

All mentees should evaluate their company's commitment to personal development. They should look around the company and see whether their peers are pursuing their own development. If they find others in the company passionately in pursuit of career advancement and recognizing that the route is through exceptional performance and contributions, then they should feel positive about their prospects within the company.

Mentees should work very closely with their managers to ensure there is a tight linkage between their personal development plans and the company's business objectives to create a synergy that delivers a competitive advantage to the company.

It will be difficult for an employee to succeed through mentoring if he or she is working in an organization that does not value leadership aspirations. It is critical that high-potential and high-aspiration individuals determine whether they are working in an environment that values people development as a core competency.

A simple way to assess an organization's environment is to look around and see whether the supervisors and other managers are involved in personal leadership development activities. When others in the organization are focused on their own personal development, their company is more likely positioned to achieve greatness. On the other hand, if there is no evidence that others in the organization are engaged in personal leadership development activities, high-aspiration employees should reassess whether this is an environment that is conducive to their personal career aspirations.

Work to Win

Mentees must also understand that winning is important. They must develop a passion for *not* losing. They must be better prepared, highly motivated, and more creative than their competitors.

To be excellent performers, mentees must seek opportunities to improve their ability to provide and receive constructive feedback that helps them improve their performance.

In business, regardless of what you might hear otherwise, the most important measure of success is winning. No one wants to work for a losing company. No one wants to work with a losing employee. Given their

CAUTION

NEVER JUSTIFY LOSING

Excellence of character usually emphasizes qualities such as integrity, courage, honesty, and loyalty. Notice: there is no reference to losing. Therefore, do not allow anyone to convince you that a pattern of losing is the way to build character. You do not need to fail in order to build character. There are more effective ways to do that.

The only value that one should gain from losing is having the opportunity to compete again. Do not justify racking up losses in the pursuit of building character. If you do, you are sure to fail.

preferences, most people would prefer to work for a company that has a team that values winning and wins consistently.

Likewise, no one wants to work for company that does not play by the rules, follow the laws, and take balanced risks to achieve success. Winning is valuable only when it is done in an honorable, respectful, and honest way. Winning at any cost is unacceptable.

For the mentee to win consistently, he or she has to craft a partnership with a mentor who helps him or her define the right career strategy.

Show the Courage to Lead

Mentees who are interested in expanding their leadership responsibilities will usually be received favorably. Colleagues are likely to be impressed by their courage to step up to a leadership position and willingness to provide guidance and direction for the rest of the team.

High-aspiration individuals have a passion for developing as leaders. They do not see anything inherently wrong or undesirable about wanting to earn the opportunity to lead. However, having a passion to earn the right to be developed does not give anyone the right to be developed at the expense of others.

Being selected as a mentee, formally or informally, should be viewed as a privilege. However, being selected as a mentee does not guarantee accelerated personal advancement. To succeed, mentees must excel in their careers and significantly outperform their peers. They must be more passionate about their work and consistently deliver outstanding results.

In addition to continuing to deliver outstanding performance, mentees must build win-win relationships within their organizations.

Most important, they need to have a partnership with their immediate supervisor. When mentees fail to develop effective relationships with their immediate supervisor, the difficulty in achieving significant career advancement increases substantially.

Set Great Expectations

Organizations will seldom achieve much more than they expect. When a company does not expect, encourage, and inspire great performance from its employees, it most likely will never achieve great performance itself. Accordingly, when a company does not expect great performance of itself, it can jeopardize the future of its employees, because it will be difficult to inspire the team to deliver great results.

Likewise, when an employee is reluctant to seek and/or value constructive feedback regarding his or her performance, he or she contributes to making the organization less effective. Employees should help the organization set the pace for success.

Again, mentoring should be reserved for those people who are pursuing a great goal or who believe that they should be. High-aspiration and high-potential mentees are not embarrassed by their desire to play a leadership role in their organizations. They want to be held responsible for delivering results.

All employees should feel obligated to seriously consider entering into a mentoring relationship. This includes those who consistently operate at peak performance and see no opportunity for improvement.

If mentoring programs are so important to the organization and the employee, why have so few organizations incorporated them into their personal development programs? Enlightened organizations seek opportunities to mitigate the risk of losing talent by constructively engaging each employee in a process to improve his or her contributions in the company. Mentoring is one of several ways for managers to demonstrate their commitment to excellence.

* * *

In the final few chapters, we will briefly review some of the advantages and disadvantages of mentoring based on gender and culture. Also, we will offer some suggestions on finding the right mentors, such as professional mentors, and summarize earlier discussions regarding when mentoring relationships should begin and how long they should last. Finally, we will highlight potential problems that may arise in a mentoring relationship.

Manager's Checklist for Chapter 10

☒ Determine what type of mentoring relationship would be most valuable to you.

☒ Clearly define your long-term career aspirations.

☒ Decide if you want mentoring to be a critical part of your long-term personal career plan.

☒ Determine what you want from a mentor.

☒ Decide if you prefer to select your mentor or have one assigned to you by the organization.

☒ Understand if your organization expects you to do great things.

☒ Reflect on your current work environment and assess whether your management encourages you to do great things.

☒ Make sure you believe that your organization leaders inspire you to do great things.

☒ Revisit any experiences you may have from previous mentoring relationships.

☒ Make sure that you are prepared to allocate the appropriate time and commitment to a mentoring program.

☒ Determine the type of mentoring program you would you prefer to participate in.

☒ Decide how important it is, and does it matter, if your organization implements a formal mentoring program.

☒ Consider the potential advantages of engaging a professional mentor with or without your organization's support.

Cross-Culture and Cross-Gender Mentoring

Trust and confidence establish the baseline for a successful mentoring relationship. Whether these relationships are established by individuals (self-selected) or initiated through a corporate matchmaking program, the trust and confidence will likely be assumed simply because of the profiles of the individuals involved.

Focus on Performance

To earn and maintain the confidence of their employees, management has to demonstrate a sense of fairness and accountability. Employees are more likely to deliver outstanding performance when they believe their managers will support their efforts and reward them accordingly for their contributions. In other words, management must emphasize a sense of fairness and equity throughout the organization, rewarding employees based on their performance and contributions rather than their personal profiles, to earn the confidence and trust of all employees.

Most employees understand the relationship between risk and reward. Therefore, to earn the confidence of each person, management has to create an environment where employees understand and value the risk associated with their work. It is important to note that prudent risk is valued. Conversely, self-centered behavior, resulting in excessive or reckless risk, should never be encouraged or tolerated.

The Impact on Performance: The Diversity Challenge

It is understandable, based on the diversity challenges within many organizations, that women may more readily trust other women, simply because of their gender relationships. The same is true for men. Likewise, people from a particular ethnic background might trust others from the same background more readily than someone from a different cultural experience.

From a historical perspective, women, members of minorities, and recent immigrants are more likely to have less trust and confidence in the organizations in which they work. This issue is based on the fact that most managers in most organizations are not women, members of minorities, or recent immigrants.

As a result, many women, members of minorities, and recent immigrants will seek alignment with people within the organization who are similar to them in personal backgrounds simply because they offer them the most comfort. Unfortunately, often the places where they seek the most comfort are not necessarily the places that will provide them the greatest opportunity for personal career growth.

Typical Patterns for Establishing a Mentoring Relationship

The basis for establishing an effective relationship between mentee and mentor is some common experience and expectations. Therefore, it might seem most effective, for example, for women to seek other women as mentors. Similarly, an African-American mentee might have more trust and confidence in a mentor who shares the same heritage. In certain situations, these options may be the obvious path to pursue. For example, historical patterns reveal that men typically will serve as mentors for other men and women are more likely to mentor other women.

However, as we will discuss later, an employee should not assume that getting a mentor of the same gender or a shared ethnic background will allow for the most effective mentoring relationship. The same is true for members of any other homogeneous group.

The employee must understand that more value will be gained from a mentoring relationship if he or she is honest and forthright about his or her career aspirations and current performance. This should help determine the type of individual who should serve as a mentor, whether the mentor should be of the same gender, ethnicity, or background. Each situation will be unique based on the employee's personal preferences, career goals, and work environment.

The mentor will add substantially more value to the relationship if he or she shares personal experiences and insights with which the mentee can relate. Furthermore, open dialogue is absolutely necessary for the mentor to understand as much about the mentee as possible in order to provide the highest level of support. However, it is not necessary for the mentor to provide the same level of insight and perspective, from his or her own experiences, as he or she expects the mentee to share. The simple reason is that the mentee is there to seek the help of the mentor. While an effective mentor will gain substantially from the experience with the mentee, usually the mentor is not seeking advice from the mentee.

Matchmaking Process

As discussed in previous chapters, there are basically three ways to establish a mentoring relationship. The organization assigns a specific mentor to an employee, an employee seeks out a specific mentor of choice, and a mentor identifies a particular employee whom he or she would like to mentor.

When organizations assign mentors to mentees, they have an opportunity to influence the cultural, gender, and age considerations in the relationship. However, before people begin matching mentors to mentees, they should clearly define the rationale and the logic that will be used when determining which mentors should be matched with which mentees. Once the matching scheme has been established, the people responsible for matching must ensure that each match meets the established matching criteria.

Certainly there are logical reasons why management may immediately assume that an employee in the engineering department should be mentored by someone with an engineering background. One can also understand why a salesperson may perceive it to be more valuable to be mentored by a sales manager than by someone from the human resources department. However, I am not sure if that is always necessary or even in the best interests of the employee at any time.

Nonetheless, once management has defined the guidelines for building these partnerships, they should be communicated broadly throughout the organization. In other words, if management is going to play the role of matchmaker, then all parties should know the rules of engagement.

When mentoring relationships are established by either someone seeking mentoring or someone interested in mentoring, the rules for establishing the relationship are determined by the individual initiating the engagement. Most likely these mentoring relationships will be informal.

Cross-Gender Mentoring

The foundation of all mentoring relationships will be the trust and confidence the partners have in each other. In this regard, there will be situations and occasions when female employees will prefer to partner with female mentors. This decision should be determined by the mentee.

Management should be sensitive to the needs of all mentees. Therefore, if a female employee would prefer a female mentor, management should try to accommodate her preference.

While management should work to meet the needs of the mentee, in general, it should neither encourage nor discourage woman-to-woman

CAUTION

MALE MENTORS VS. FEMALE MENTORS

As reported by Connie Glaser, a leading expert on gender communication and women's leadership issues and author of *GenderTalk Works: 7 Steps for Cracking the Gender Code at Work*, some researchers believe that gender matters when seeking a mentor. This research implies that the mentee's choice should depend on what he or she is looking for in the relationship.

Further, Glaser reports that, according to a study conducted by Professors John S. Sosik and Veronica M. Godshalk of Pennsylvania State University, female mentors appear to be better role models than men. However, the study suggests that male mentors are more effective at leading the way to the top of the organization (*www.divinecaroline.com/article/22278/44829-male-vs-female-which-mentor*).

mentoring relationships. Unless specifically requested, all mentoring relationships should be gender-blind unless there are specific situations in which a same-gender match would yield substantial better results for the mentee.

In most organizations, the majority of managers are white males. However, with the global dynamics in business, the mix is changing. Today, women outnumber men in the U.S. workforce. In addition, they are assuming more management positions in their organizations.

Too often, women new to an organization tend to associate primarily with other women in the organization at the expense of building relationships with men as well. Instead, they should seek the opportunity to partner with the leaders within their organizations. Therefore, since men hold most of the senior positions in business, women should be encouraged to partner with male mentors as well as female mentors. Mentees should try to remain gender-neutral in selecting mentors.

Certainly, women and men are different. In general, women deal with different issues than do men. One adversity, or complexity, of cross-gender mentoring relationships is the historical scarcity of role-modeling functions within business. During the early years of their careers, women will face similar types of obstacles as men. However, women face some problems that are unique to being female in male dominated organizations.

THE KIDS

FOR EXAMPLE

Generally, a working mother is more likely than a working father to be affected by the need to be home with a sick child. Also, a working woman who is planning to give birth will have a unique set of challenges that men do not have to deal with directly.

Of course, today it is common for the working father to be home for family reasons. However, working men will never have to deal with the challenges of actually giving birth.

Cross-Culture Mentoring

It is important for all employees to understand how to effectively integrate into a business environment. Whether they are members of minorities, members of the majority, or recent immigrants, it is important that all employees broaden their base of activities throughout their organizations.

Just like women, too often new employees who are members of minorities and other ethnic groups tend to associate primarily with others in the organization who are of the same or similar cultures at the expense of building relationships with people who are different. Too frequently, members of minorities will migrate toward communities within the organizations with which they are more historically aligned. While it should be understandable, as mentioned earlier, that tendency may not necessarily be the most effective way for them to capitalize on the opportunities within their firms.

MINORITY MANAGERS

FOR EXAMPLE

Members of most minority groups, including African Americans, Asian Americans, and Latinos, are underrepresented in management and executive positions within U.S. corporations. Progress is being made, but there is still a need for substantial improvement. For instance, research in 2004 showed that the Hispanic population in the United States, including Puerto Rico, exceeded 43 million. Further, it was estimated that the Latino population is growing by nearly 2 million each year. However, while this group is growing in size and representation within the workforce, Latino professionals represent less than 4 percent of that population. Furthermore, they represent less than 2 percent of corporate board members and less than 1 percent of corporate executives ("Hispanics in Corporate America," Donna Maria Blancero and Robert G. DelCampo, *Hispanic MBA*, December 2004, *www.multiculturaladvantage.com/ contentmgt/ anmviewer.asp?a=668&z=4&isasp*).

Frequently, throughout my career, I have seen African-American employees focus most of their activities around other African Americans within their companies. The same can be said for other ethnic groups, such as Asians Americans and Hispanic Americans.

Again, I suggest that mentees broaden their networks as well as broaden their levels of engagement in such a way that they expose themselves to communities within the organization that, in addition to supporting their efforts are in a position to help grow and develop. In other words, cross-cultural mentoring relationships can benefit both the mentee and the mentor.

I am not suggesting that members of minorities or women abandon the communities with which they feel comfortable. However, I am sug-

---

CULTURAL LITERACY FOR MENTORS

"For mentors to be effective across cultures they must be culturally literate and be sensitive to the needs of individuals from different cultural backgrounds," according to Zulfi Hussein, co-founder of the European Mentoring and Coaching Council, in "Mentoring Across Cultures" (in *Techniques for Coaching and Mentoring*, ed. David Megginson and David Clutterbuck, Butterworth-Heinemann, 2005). Having "cultural literacy," he explains, means understanding the values, beliefs, and symbols of the dominant culture, other cultures, and the workplace and how those values, beliefs, and symbols are reflected in assumptions and behaviors.

---

gesting that they broaden their relationships and their networks to have a richer experience that will have a much more positive impact on their personal career growth. Zulfi Hussein sums up the benefits for both parties in "Mentoring Across Cultures": "Cross-cultural mentoring provides an ideal opportunity to enhance the understanding of different cultures for both mentors and mentees. It also promotes learning for both partners on how to communicate across cultures."

Summary

In summary, it is more important for mentees to select mentors who can provide the most significant support in their efforts to achieve their personal career aspirations. Therefore, at times mentoring relationships might take some mentees out of their comfort zones.

Mentees should seek mentors who satisfy their mentoring requirements. Therefore, if a woman believes that a female mentor would be in her best interests at any given time, she should seek one without reservation. The same is true for members of minorities and other ethnic groups, as well as for those who prefer to be mentored by someone from within their functional organizations.

Fortunately, there are increasingly more women, members of minorities, and recent immigrants in significant positions in business. As a result, over time, there will be less need for the mentee or mentor selection process to focus on gender and cultural sensitivities. However, today it is still an important consideration for all.

In the next chapter we are going to discuss when employees and employers should seek the opportunity to enter into mentoring relationships.

Manager's Checklist for Chapter 11

☑ Decide if you are comfortable recommending male mentors for female mentees.

☑ Determine if you would you be comfortable suggesting a female mentor for a female mentee.

☑ Consider if you would you support an individual from sales being mentored by someone from an engineering department or vice-versa.

☑ Develop your position regarding gender-centered mentoring relationships.

☑ Evaluate your organizations' sensitivity to the homogeneity-heterogeneity mentoring issue.

☑ Assess your organizations' enthusiasm to embrace multi-ethnic mentoring.

☑ Anticipate your employees likely preference to a culture-centric approach to mentoring (e.g., African American to African American, Asian American to Asian American, etc.).

Seeking a Mentor/ Duration of Relationship

Throughout this book, we've emphasized the importance of mentoring. We have discussed the significant advantages of effective mentoring programs. Whether it's informal or formal, we've seen the value of mentoring for any organization.

Management

Managers should incorporate their mentoring programs and strategies into the overall strategic planning processes for their businesses. However, managers should not wait for the new planning cycle before they revisit, revamp, or begin implementing the mentoring process. There is no value in waiting. If managers believe that mentoring will help develop their leaders, they should make mentoring a part of their businesses as soon as possible.

When managers hire employees, it's just the beginning. New employees will be joining veteran employees on a continuous learning curve. The old saying that people are our most important resource is true. So when employees fail to grow and develop, organizations risk failure.

The mentoring process for all new employees should be evaluated and management should determine if mentoring is appropriate for each of them. High-aspiration and high-potential employees should be introduced to some form of mentoring program as soon as possible. All other employees should be mentored as management deems appropri-

SMART MANAGING

ELIMINATING THE BARRIERS

Managers must successfully integrate new hires entering into their organizations. They must foster a climate for each protégé to reach his or her full potential by helping to identify and eliminate barriers to effective performance and career success.

According to the American Society of Mechanical Engineers Professional Practice Curriculum (*www.professionalpractice.asme.org/transition/mentoring/2.htm*), managers must use mentoring to achieve the following:

- Transition new employees into the workplace.
- Transmit the organizational culture.
- Develop technical experts who are capable of assuming managerial roles.
- Transmit needed skills.
- Enhance career development of employees.
- Improve the workplace climate.
- Facilitate diversity awareness.
- Engage more staff in developing new employees.
- Improve the lines of communication.

ate, based on their interest and the organization's capacity to provide mentoring.

Managers should not have the opportunity to opt out of their leadership development responsibilities. Therefore, mentoring should be considered, and included as appropriate, as part of management's plans for effectively developing all employee talent. From a management perspective, mentoring should be an ongoing process. Managers should continually seek appropriate mentoring opportunities for their employees. Managers should understand that mentoring is simply a part of their responsibilities as organizational leaders.

Employees

Mentoring offers such compelling advantages to an employee that he or she should seek a mentor as soon as possible. However, the benefits of mentoring for an employee will vary according to many factors, such as the duration and formal structure of the relationship. Also, an employee should use different types of mentoring at different times during his or her career.

As discussed above, many new employees need help to effectively integrate into their organizations. Mentoring is a good way to provide the support they will need. Likewise, many employees will need help when they take on new job responsibilities. Again, mentoring is a good way to provide the assistance they will need. And certainly high-aspiration and high-potential employees will need assistance in developing strategic work activities that align their personal career aspirations with the needs of the organization. Once again, mentoring is a good way to deliver the support they will need.

When an employee becomes serious about his or her career aspirations, it is the right time to get help. That is why I encourage all high-aspiration and high-potential employees to seek a mentor as soon as feasible. When an employee seeks mentoring, it will often be determined by his or her experience and/or particular need at a certain time.

TAKE CHARGE

TRICKS OF THE TRADE

In "Mentoring: An Age Old Idea Whose Time Has Come" (*Canadian Manager*, December 22, 2001), Shawn Kent offers the following advice for employees who want to benefit from mentoring:

- Show a desire to learn.
- Be specific about what you want to learn.
- Assess your abilities and weaknesses.
- Set clear goals.
- Find people who are doing what you want to do or who know what you need to know next.
- Show the qualities that attract mentors: intelligence, ambition, loyalty, commitment, ability to work with others, and desire to accept responsibilities and take risks.
- Begin working toward a mentoring relationship by inviting the person to breakfast or lunch.
- Pay attention to your mentor and be sensitive to ways in which you can help him or her.

For example, in some cases, early career mentoring may be provided by a member of the employee's family. In other cases, it might be provided by a colleague through a peer-to-peer relationship. Yet, for some employees, it may be better to engage directly with a professional mentor very early in the career planning cycle.

All employees within the organization should seek the opportunity to discuss the concept of mentoring with their immediate supervisors. In particular, new employees in the organization should discuss the concept of mentoring with their supervisor. They need help in developing their short-term and long-term personal career plans. These plans should incorporate some form of mentoring as deemed appropriate by the employee. Furthermore, the employee's personal career plan should be inextricably linked with his or her personal performance plan.

Summarizing so far, employees who believe that mentoring is an effective process to build and enhance personal connections should find a mentor immediately. It is a great way to promote professional vitality within the organization and their industry.

Managers who believe that effective mentoring can improve retention, build morale, and increase commitment while accelerating leadership development and providing career advancement should also begin implementing mentoring programs immediately.

Since mentoring provides such significant advantages to both managers and employees, both should seek opportunities to start now. The sooner they start, the sooner they will realize the benefits.

Now that we know when to seek a mentor, we will discuss how long a mentoring relationship should last.

How Long Should Mentoring Last?

Before the mentoring partnership is established, all parties must have shared expectations regarding the duration of the program. That is, how long should the mentoring partnership last? Clarity is paramount; there should be no room for ambiguity.

Since we have briefly addressed this question in several previous chapters, at this time we will simply provide a brief summary. Our intent is to synthesize some of our earlier points into a single synopsis.

In general, there are no specific rules regarding the duration of a mentoring program. The term of the relationship is to be established by the parties involved. A mentoring relationship should last as long as necessary to help the mentee achieve his or her stated goals.

Formal Corporate Mentoring

What about the duration of formal corporate mentoring. Let's look at it for new employees and tenured employees.

New Employees

Mentoring relationships that are designed to help integrate new employees into an organization are likely to be short. If the on-boarding process is part of a formal corporate mentoring program, it will likely last no more than 90 days.

However, if the mentoring relationship is informal and the participants choose to work together, the relationship is likely to last until the mentee achieves a level of status at which the mentor no longer adds substantial advantage or feels the need or obligation to provide continuing support.

> **On-boarding process**
> Process of accelerating the assimilation of employees, whether they are new to the organization or moving from one department into another. It is a prerequisite to getting the organization successfully organized and aligned around its needs.
>
> **KEY TERM**

Tenured Employees

Formal corporate mentoring programs for employees with experience in the organization should last no less than six months and no more than 18. These time frames will allow the mentee ample time to ben-

> **MAKE SURE YOU'RE GETTING THE RESULTS YOU WANT**
>
> **SMART MANAGING**
>
> The sooner employees are integrated into their new roles, the sooner they will be able to contribute to the success of the organization. Therefore, the effects of the on-boarding process should be quantified and measured. There should be a positive correlation between effective on-boarding and the success of the department and the organization.

efit from the relationship with the experienced mentor. Also, if the mentoring relationship lasts no longer than 18 months, the mentee will have more time to apply what he or she has learned from the relationship and to partner with other mentors. As a result, the mentee will not be limited to the experiences and teaching of one mentor. Instead, he or she will have the opportunity, over time, to learn and benefit from the experiences of several.

Professional Mentoring

As emphasized during our discussion regarding professional mentors, they will offer a broader selection of program options for the mentee to consider. Each program option will likely have a different duration.

Professional mentoring programs should last at least as long as it takes the mentors to help the mentees develop plans and objectives to achieve their long-term career aspirations. However, it is not necessary for the mentor to continue the relationship until the mentee actually achieves those long-term objectives.

In general, professional mentors should be considered when the mentoring is expected to last no less than three months and no more than two years. Because professional mentors are independent of management and the organization, they are able to support multiple mentees concurrently, with the relationships varying in duration.

NEEDS-BASED DURATIONS
FOR EXAMPLE

XCEO, Inc. offers mentees four unique program options. The duration of each program is matched against the mentee's personal career objectives.

Each program (silver, gold, gold plus, and specialized) has unique characteristics. They vary according to duration, ranging from three months to two years. They also vary according to the number of engagements between the mentor and the protégé and the length of each engagement.

To provide ultimate flexibility and a broad range of offerings, XCEO also offers several self- paced mentoring program options (*www.xceo.net/mentoring*).

KEY TERM

Self-paced professional mentoring XCEO advocates extreme personal leadership as the foundation for competing effectively by inspiring creativity and leveraging intellectual capacity. XCEO designed the Self-Paced Professional Mentoring Program to advance individual careers by emphasizing personal development. The program is self-directed and includes tools to help individuals develop high-performance personal career plans, which are inextricably linked to their personal performance plans.

The objective of the self-paced mentoring program is to accelerate the pace of development for high-potential individuals. Engaging the principles of extreme personal leadership is the most effective method for maximizing results (*www.xceo.net/mentoring/sp.php*).

Informal Mentoring

Like formal mentoring programs, informal mentoring programs are likely to have varying durations, too. They can last from as little as one month to a lifetime.

When individuals self-select to participate in an informal mentoring relationship, obviously they will determine how long they desire their relationship to last. However, there is a difference between a lasting relationship and an effective mentoring partnership. Long-term informal mentoring relationships are likely to evolve into friendships. As this transition occurs, it is likely that the friendship will produce substantially less benefit for the mentee than a real mentoring partnership. Again, mentoring relationships should be dissolved when they are no longer effective.

As we have discussed, there are differences between informal corporate mentoring and broad-based informal mentoring. These relationships, such as peer-to-peer mentoring and friends and family mentoring, will tend to last longer than informal mentoring on the job. Peer-to-peer mentoring will typically have a short duration, six months or less. Friends and family mentoring is likely to last a lifetime.

Managers should be very sensitive when discussing with employees the durations of informal mentoring programs that are not sponsored by the corporation. These self-selected informal mentoring programs are more akin to friendships and therefore likely to be more susceptible to emotional implications than programs sanctioned by the organization.

Manager's Checklist for Chapter 12

☑ Decide if you have sufficient time to devote to mentoring an employee.

☑ Determine if some of your employees have sufficient time to participate in a mentoring program.

☑ Decide if now is the right time to implement a formal mentoring program within your organization.

☑ Assess your organizations' readiness to implement a formal mentoring program at this time.

☑ Consider if this might not be the best time to implement a formal mentoring program within your organization.

☑ Decide how you will ensure that employee job performance is not adversely impacted by the duration of their mentoring relationships.

☑ Work closely with employees to align the duration of their mentoring programs with their long-term personal career aspirations.

☑ Do not allow short-term performance objectives to be perceived as obviating the need for mentoring programs of longer duration.

☑ Organize your mentoring programs so the duration does not compromise the success of the organization.

How to Find and Hire a Mentor

Why You Should Hire a Professional Mentor

Professional mentoring provides distinct advantages over all other forms of mentoring programs. When employees and managers partner with professional mentors, they capitalize on their independence and a broader range of experiences. When these mentors are engaged as part of the overall corporate leadership development activities, they are likely to be more objective and offer perspectives beyond the corporate experiences.

Professional mentors will function most effectively when they are engaged with high-aspiration and high-potential employees who are eager to implement plans and strategies that accelerate them toward achieving their long-term personal career aspirations, while maximizing their contributions to the company. Professional mentors have a passion for excellence and they inspire their protégés to strive for the same. Organizations should view them as an extension of their leadership development team.

Organizations that value leadership as a core competency offer comprehensive programs to support their employee development activities. These activities may include formal corporate mentoring, executive coaching, leadership training, university management development programs, and so on. The highly enlightened organizations will consider professional mentoring as an additional option to broaden their leadership development offerings.

Leaders and Motivation

For decades, researchers have attempted to discover how leaders motivate their followers. James MacGregor Burns, in his book, *Leadership* (Harper Collins, 1978), theorized that leadership behaviors fall into one of two broad categories, which he called *transactional* and *transformational*.

Burns argued that transactional leaders influence people by appealing to their self-interest. They offer something of interest in exchange for the performance they desire, such as money, status, or favors. Often, they also set punishments in case they do not get the performance they desire.

In contrast, transformational leaders inspire others to higher levels of motivation. Transformational leadership is built on shared values and teamwork. It is primarily people-oriented leadership.

KEY TERMS

Transactional leader One who leads solely or primarily through the use of rewards and/or punishment. Transactional leadership is built on reciprocity; leadership power is based on position within a hierarchy.

This type of leadership is more aligned with corporate formal mentoring programs. In this environment, mentors have the ability to influence how the mentees are rewarded and/or punished based on their performances.

Transformational leader One who influences others by empowering and elevating them. Transformational leaders believe that leaders and followers can raise each other to higher levels of motivation and morality. Transformational leaders influence not only their followers, but also their peers and even their own leaders.

Professional mentors do not have the option or desire to function in a transactional leadership role. They do not reward or punish their mentees. They inspire high-aspiration individuals to pursue and achieve the highest levels of their capabilities.

Professional Mentors as Extreme Personal Leaders

World-class professional mentors are extreme personal leaders who ascend to the next higher level of leadership. They move transformational leadership to a broader platform by working with their mentees to help them identify their visions and the ability to articulate them clearly. They help their mentees discover justifiable reasons to develop and maintain a positive attitude about their future and the future of their organization. Further, they encourage their mentees to dream up innovative approaches to accelerate their personal performance.

When professional mentors perform as extreme personal leaders, they do more than simply encourage individuals to elevate themselves; they encourage them to work with entire groups to accept their visions and to work toward the goals demanded by those visions. To propel themselves and other people to act in ways that elevate, professional mentors partner with their mentees to link great ideas to inspiring images of success.

A professional mentor will provide a plan tailored specifically to an individual's needs. Hiring a professional mentor to provide services to an employee should be considered as an attractive alternative to using a formal mentor from within the organization. These professional mentors are difficult to find and typically will require an investment by the organization on behalf of the employee. However, engaging a successful professional mentor is more likely to produce substantial results for the mentee.

As highlighted earlier in this chapter, professional mentors offer significant advantages to both the employee and the employer.

The mentor should bring a perspective to the employee without concern of a potential conflict of interest. The mentor should relieve the employee of any concerns of potential retaliation. In addition, the mentor should help the employee explore all options relative to his or her short- and long-term career aspirations.

The professional mentor provides advantages to the employer, too. First of all, the mentor relieves the corporate formal mentor of concerns of conflict of interest. The mentor will work on behalf of the employee, but he or she will balance those interests with the needs of the organization. Also, the mentor will be concerned about maintaining the respect and support of other members of the team. However, it is likely they will not even know that the mentor has a relationship with any employee, whereas they would certainly know if a corporate formal mentor were providing similar support to the employees and it could cause those who are not being mentored to consider themselves at a disadvantage.

Professional mentoring should be viewed as a complementary program. When managers develop their strategies for leadership development, professional mentoring should be considered as one of the options. Next, let's discuss a few of the best ways to find the right mentor.

How to Find a Mentor

Throughout this book, we have reiterated the importance of matching the right mentor with the right mentee. Again, this is one of the more critical decisions to be made before initiating a mentoring relationship. As a result, before management, or the mentee, begins looking for a mentor, they should have a reasonably good idea of what they are looking for.

The mentor search process will vary according to who is leading the search. When managers seek mentors for their employees, they are likely to follow a different strategy than an individual personally seeking a mentor. Again, one of the more important, and early, steps in the management-initiated selection process is to understand the needs and desires of the mentee. In other words, managers should understand the needs of their clients.

Management Initiated

For the mentoring program to be successful, it is important that the employee and the supervisor agree on the mentoring support to be offered. Further, managers should include the employees when determining the type of mentoring program. Also, the employee's engagement is critically important when determining the appropriate mentoring candidates.

SMART MANAGING

ONE STEP AT A TIME

The following outline suggests some basic steps to consider when developing a process to identify the right mentors for a successful mentoring program.

1. Define the importance of mentoring within the organization.
2. Define the mentoring capacity of the organization.
3. Identify the prospective mentees within the organization.
4. Define the needs of the mentees.
5. Determine whether the organization will pursue a formal or informal mentoring relationship.
6. Determine the type of formal or informal mentoring program.
7. Find the right mentor.

Another early step in the mentor search process is determining what type of mentor should be pursued. This is important because the strategy for pursuing a formal mentor is substantially different than pursuing an informal one. Also, there should be different strategies for the different types of formal mentors, and likewise, varying strategies for the different informal mentors.

When managers seek mentors for their formal corporate mentoring programs they should look for executives who are in positions that are most likely to benefit their mentees. These individuals should be the role models within the organization.

The high-aspiration and high-potential employees should be matched with the most senior people within the organization who are participating in the mentoring program. Managers must be students of the organization. In other words, they must understand the route to the top. With this understanding, managers will be able to identify those executives who will be the most valuable mentors for their employees.

Find out how people are developed. Learn the rules of the game. To be effective, managers must understand how the company works and how they can leverage their knowledge and personal relationships to assist their employees in their pursuit of their long-term career aspirations.

TRACK THE WINNERS *TRICKS OF THE TRADE*

Managers should learn where the successful people in the company gained their experiences. If they are in the company's accounting division and want to help their employees, or themselves, to become the chief financial officer (CFO), they should learn what key jobs the present CFO had before he or she ascended to that position.

While they are at it, they should find out what positions the controller previously held, on the way. Track the career paths of the successful individuals who high-aspiration and high-potential employees should be interested in mirroring.

Managers should understand the company's organization chart and where the influence and power are located. That is how they find the best mentors for their people.

FRIEND OR FOE?

CAUTION Managers should not be fooled into believing that people in positions that are similar to their employees (i.e., peer competitors) are eager to see them advance. Some employees really do not care whether these employees, or you for that matter, advance at all.

Be acutely aware of this! It is vital that high-aspiration and high-potential employees are aware that they will have to navigate around the will of people who do not care if they succeed, or who do not want them to succeed. Managers and mentees should seek mentors who have a broad base of employee support throughout the organization. That is where you will most likely find the best mentors.

Mentee Initiated

When mentees search for mentors, through a self-selection process, they are likely to already have a general understanding of their needs. As a result, there is at least one less step in their search process.

As we have discussed in previous chapters, it is important for managers to determine whether they want to a mentor someone. They should decide if they want to mentor someone within their organization or perhaps mentor someone outside their immediate organization. They will not find the best mentors for their employees within their own departments.

Equally as important, the mentees must decide whether they want to be mentored by someone within the company or from outside of the company. If they choose to be mentored by someone within the company, they must further decide whether to be mentored by their immediate supervisor or by someone outside of the organization.

Mentees must decide what they want to be and who they want to identify with and strive to emulate. This is important because an effective mentor will make a substantial difference in how mentees progress toward achieving their long-term career aspirations.

When management provides mentorship for the employee, without being solicited by the employee to provide such services, then the employer should play a larger role in the selection process. However, if the mentee initiates the discussion regarding a potential mentor, then the mentee is most likely to be the driver in determining whom he or she would prefer as a mentor.

If an employee approaches his or her supervisor, and asks to be mentored by the CEO of the company, the supervisor might conclude that at this stage of the employee's career it would be inappropriate for the CEO to be a mentor. Perhaps, the CEO has no interest in providing mentorship for this particular individual. Given this scenario, management should offer alternative candidates for the employee to consider.

Likewise, if management offers a mentor, such as the CFO of the company, to provide mentorship for an employee, the employee might conclude that given his or her individual career aspirations, the CFO function is not one that will be most valuable to his or her career pursuits.

Having the wrong mentor could in fact be more detrimental to an employee's career than having no mentor at all. Therefore it is important that management and the employee allocate sufficient time in understanding the implications of engaging in a relationship with a mentor.

Selecting a mentor is a very important step in the professional life of the mentee. In addition, it is very important each time a mentor engages with the new mentee. In some work environments, mentees may have their mentor assigned to them by the company. In other situations, the mentee will personally identify and select a mentor.

Some researchers believe the most powerful mentor will be selected by the mentee for the express purpose of the learning and career-advancement. They believe this to be true because, ideally, a trusted adviser who provides both support and inspiration is critical. The mentee and mentor relationship is a psychosocial as well as a professional relationship.

When a mentor is sourced from within the organization it could result in a great experience. On the other hand it is just as likely to result in a bad experience. Managers provide experience and proficiency that may be most valuable to the employee. In some regard, the mentoring role may seem second nature to the supervisor. He or she may be able to directly impact the performance of the whole organization through a single successful mentoring relationship (C. Mason & E. Bailey, *Benefits and Pitfalls of Mentoring*, STC 50th Annual Conference Proceedings).

However, the previous situation may not always turn out so favorably. To the contrary, if the mentoring relationship does not go as well as expected it could have a devastating negative impact on the organization. As we discussed in an earlier chapter, mentoring and managing do not necessarily go together.

During a career, it is likely that an employee will have several mentors. The type of mentor will be determined by the specific needs of the employee at a particular stage of his or her career. It is also very likely that an employee may have several mentors concurrently. As we discussed earlier, there are formal and informal relationships. While it is not likely that a mentee will have multiple formal mentors at the same time, it is reasonable to assume that he or she may have several informal mentors in tandem. Furthermore, many employees will have an informal mentor, such as a friend or family member, while participating in a formal mentoring program at the same time.

There are several sources to be considered when managers or employees seek the services of a professional mentor. Obviously, in today's connected world, the Internet provides a plethora of resources to be considered. However, managers and employees should invest substantial time to locate the professional mentor who best meets their needs. While there are plenty professional mentoring sites on the web, there are substantially less outstanding professional mentors available. Professional mentors who provide leadership products and services based on experience and research are more likely to be the most effective ones for consideration.

Once the professional mentor has been identified through the Internet, word-of-mouth references, or any other reliable sources, a personal meeting should be arranged to interview the prospective partner. Pay close attention to the credentials of the professional mentor. Make sure they have the appropriate experiences, training, and development to deliver the services you expect with the highest level of quality. Professional mentors should have a portfolio of work experiences, research and, ideally, published works to substantiate their existence.

When mentees are looking for an informal mentoring relationship, they will have no difficulty finding mentors among their friends and families. In these environments, the mentees should look for individuals who can have the most favorable influence on their personal career aspirations rather than partnering with someone whom they care about. Further, mentees should seek to meet people within their profession and industry. Work to identify with people who have achieved what they would like to achieve. However, mentees must remain mindful that mentoring is a serious business process. It is not a network designed for building friendships.

When mentees seek mentors from within the corporation, the corporate intranet is a very valuable tool. Similar to using the Internet, mentees should scour the company's web site to identify individuals who they believe will be receptive to partnering with them and be able to provide the type of partnership that will result in advancement toward their personal career objectives. Also, mentees should work directly with their managers to seek recommendations of the individuals who might be willing to serve as their mentors.

Peer-to-peer mentors are much less difficult to locate. They are readily available and most often willing, and sometimes eager to serve as mentors for while. They respond favorably to management's request, as well as the mentee's excitement, when approached to serve in a mentoring capacity. When an employee identifies a peer who would make an effective mentor, he or she should not hesitate to approach and ask for help.

In summary, the best way to find a mentor is to search all of the sources available. Talk to your friends and family, peers and supervisors, people within your industry and search the Internet until you find the person who meets your needs.

In the concluding chapter, we will highlight some of the potential pitfalls when participating in a mentoring relationship.

Manager's Checklist for Chapter 13

☑ Do you believe your high-aspiration and high-potential employees are receiving the appropriate level of mentoring?

☑ Could you use additional mentoring support to help your employees achieve their long-term personal career objectives?

☑ Are your corporate formal mentors just as effective as you perceive professional mentors to be?

☑ Would you consider redistributing some of your department assets in order to hire a professional mentor as part of your leadership development program?

☑ Has a professional mentor contributed to your personal success?

☑ Are you willing to invest in yourself by hiring a professional mentor?

☑ Are you willing to invest in your employees by hiring a professional mentor for them?

☑ Clearly define the top five requirements you would expect your mentors to meet.

☑ Define the criteria for selecting a mentor from candidates that meet all of your requirements.

☑ Determine how many mentors are needed to support your organization.

☑ Select the top five employees to participate in your next mentoring program.

☑ Decide how you plan to announce your new mentoring focus to your organization.

Concluding Thoughts on Mentoring

Potential Pitfalls

Throughout this book we have discussed the value of mentoring programs. We've reviewed the advantages that mentoring offers to the organization as well as the benefits derived by the individual. But so far, we haven't discussed what some may view as the dark side of mentoring.

Much of the literature available today, justifiably emphasizes the importance and value of mentoring. In this closing chapter we'll discuss some of the potential pitfalls of mentoring.

Implementing an effective mentoring program can be difficult. Similar to other major investment programs, it requires proper planning and effective execution. Therefore, at times managers involved in establishing a mentoring program may become discouraged. However, regardless of the challenges in pursuit of building an exciting and rewarding mentoring program, there are significant rewards to be gained.

When implemented properly, broad-based mentoring programs provide substantial advantages to all participants. The organization will benefit from the accelerated improvement in employee job performance. Mentored employees will see a marked improvement in their performance and expanded career opportunities. In addition, the mentors will see their mentee's blossom and grow as they use the knowledge and insight provided by him or her.

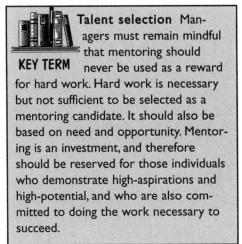

Talent selection Managers must remain mindful that mentoring should

KEY TERM never be used as a reward for hard work. Hard work is necessary but not sufficient to be selected as a mentoring candidate. It should also be based on need and opportunity. Mentoring is an investment, and therefore should be reserved for those individuals who demonstrate high-aspirations and high-potential, and who are also committed to doing the work necessary to succeed.

As rewarding as mentoring programs are for organizations and employees, there are associated risks. However, the risks are manageable, and relatively insignificant when weighed against program rewards. Nevertheless, it's important for managers to be mindful of the potential pitfalls associated with the mentoring game. Let's discuss some of the pitfalls managers should steer clear of when implementing their programs.

Mentoring Requires an Investment

First of all, mentoring is not free. In business and in life, most things that are worth having or worth doing are not free. What I want to emphasize is that developing and implementing an exciting and effective mentoring program has costs. However, it's important to view this cost as an investment, not an expense. Investing in employees should be a priority for the organization, and you should expect it to yield substantial returns for a long time.

Minimize Bureaucracy

Eliminating, or at least minimizing, bureaucracy is one of the first and significant challenges that most managers will face when implementing a mentoring program. To be effective, these programs require management's time and attention. Therefore, mentoring programs may often be perceived as interfering with the regular work required to manage the organization. In other words, mentoring could be viewed as non-value-added overhead.

So managers need to accept that mentoring programs do add some more work and require support from others in the organization. Considering the workloads required of all employees in organizations striving to be lean and efficient, typically, there is no excess capacity floating around to support a mentoring program. That doesn't mean no mentoring. It does mean that you need to consider the payoffs from the program important enough to make mentoring part of a manager's responsibilities. Managers need to remember

> **Non-value-added** Work that adds costs for the organization but no value for customers and cuts into profitability. Non-value-added activities include repairs to defective products (that shouldn't have been defective in the first place), too many management approvals, and so on. However, mentoring properly executed is definitely a *value-added* activity.
>
> **KEY TERM**

that for the mentoring process to work effectively, they must create an environment where the mentee does not view the activity as a burden on the organization and therefore get discouraged.

If this happens, those individuals not participating in the mentoring program could feel resentful, and this could have a negative effect on the overall performance of the team and organization. Further, mentees can become disenchanted with the whole process, which can result in a higher probability of increased turnover among the exact employees you don't want to lose.

Defining Employee Needs

To help employees develop, a manager must understand their weaknesses or areas they need to improve. Therefore, it's important that the relationship between a mentor and a mentee be kept confidential. For the mentor to be most effective, the employees have to be open and honest about their aspirations as well as on their current level of performance. At first it might be difficult for mentees to share this information with their mentors until they have developed a trusting and mutually respectful relationship.

Build the Right Culture

Mentoring has to be woven into the fabric of the organization for it to have a lasting impact on the success of the company. While employees may be mentored one at a time, it must be viewed as a ongoing organizational activity. Employees will come to appreciate the need for mentoring throughout their careers. Likewise, corporations will view mentoring as an important part of employee development, which will pay off for all in terms of performance and profitability.

MEASURING SUCCESS
Managers should develop specific metrics to determine the success of their mentoring programs. While there are a variety of metrics to be considered, I suggest that one of the metrics be directly tied to the economic performance of the organization. Employees who are more engaged in the company and have a direct link between their career aspirations and their performance plans are more likely to perform at a higher level and contribute more to the success of the company.

While both employees and the corporation may view the value of mentoring from their own perspectives, it must also be clear that they are in this together, and mentoring will help everyone achieve their objectives.

In other words, employees can't achieve success without partnering with the organization. And the organization will never achieve sustainable prosperity without high-performing, committed employees.

Stay Committed to Your Leadership

During difficult economic times, managers must resist the urge to reduce their investment in people development. Mentoring should never be diminished because of short-term economic difficulties. Management should view people development, such as mentoring programs, in the same light as accounting. During down times, such as well as in times of prosperity, corporations need accountants to balance the books and track the the organization's financial health. The same is true for people development. During the times of prosperity, corporations should be investing in the most critical asset in the organization—their people. And especially during difficult times investing in people is a way to ensure improved organizational performance. It also allows the organization to prepare itself to take advantage of new opportunities when economic times get better.

In today's difficult business climate, mentoring is more important than

> ## HAPPY CAMPERS
> Another key metric is the employee personal satisfaction survey. There should be a positive correlation between the level of employee satisfaction, the success of the mentoring program, and the level of performance of individuals and the organization. "Happy campers," employees who feel good about themselves, contribute more to the success of the organization.
>
> In addition, a successful mentoring program should lower the turnover rate of the highest performing and high-aspiration employees. And that's definitely good for all.

it has been in the previous two decades. One reason this is true is because most managers and employees in today's companies have never experienced a recession and the stress it puts on an organization. Mentoring by those who have is a way to help managers and employees deal with hard times intelligently and maximize their contributions to the organization.

The fact is that high-performing organizations will find creative ways to continue their mentoring programs. At a minimum, they will maintain a focus on their high-potential and high-aspiration employees. Because of this, they are more likely to maintain a higher level of morale in difficult times and have lower attrition among their highest performing people.

Conclusion

Throughout this book we've emphasized the importance of leadership development. We've stressed the importance of providing opportunities for management to leverage the effectiveness human capital throughout the organization. Mentoring is one of the most effective ways for managers to create an environment that offers continued learning opportunities for each individual resulting in improved personal job satisfaction and maximum personal contribution to organizational success.

Managers have the responsibility to deliver results from the specific tasks that they have been assigned. To improve the efficiency of the organization and its processes, employee leadership development has to be a critical part of the plan.

Sociologists have studied this for decades and have concluded that the interactions among all employees form the social system of the company. This system provides the cues that guide employee behavior and affects their motivation to perform and their commitment to success. Since managers serve as role models for employees, they have a major influence on how employees view the organization and their role in it.

Employees are more likely to follow when they are inspired rather than simply told what to do. Furthermore, employees will contribute substantially more to the success of the organization when they believed they will be rewarded for their efforts. While money is certainly an important reward to all employees there are other rewards equally or more valuable.

Employees want to feel as though they can make a meaningful contribution to the success of the organization. They want the opportunity to learn and grow and improve their value to the organization—and to themselves at the same time. An effective mentoring system helps make all this happen.

The most critical role that managers can play is leadership. Managers have fundamental responsibility for creating an environment that inspires all employees to perform at their highest levels. Management has to create an environment where employees are are both expected and want to do their jobs well, are encouraged to deliver exceptional performance, and inspired to learn and grow. And the result of this is the delivery of great products and services for customers and outstanding returns for shareholders.

Mentoring is all about helping management accomplish these goals. Mentoring should be considered an integral part of every company's leadership development program. When corporations fail to develop their high-aspiration and high-potential employees, they will fail to develop a great business.

SMART MANAGING

BE A GREAT INVESTMENT

If workers believe in the value and importance of their work, they will motivated to perform at high levels. Furthermore, workers are ready to produce more if encouraged to do so. And that encouragement most often is in the form of some reward. The opposite is also true. They will not want to contribute much when they see little or no recognition for their efforts. Here is where mentoring comes in. It is one of the most effective and efficient ways to reward employees for their contributions to the success of the organization.

Mentoring inspires smart, hard-working people to create more value for customers and more shareholder value than they would without such progams. The fact is that mentoring is a way to leverage the best talent in any organization to the benefit of all—employees, customers, and all stakeholders.

I believe that managers have a responsibility to provide opportunities for all employees to develop. They must allocate sufficient time and resources to do so effectively. When managers fail to invest in their people they fail to invest in their companies and put shareholder value at risk.

Mentoring programs provide an opportunity for management to help employees increase their value to the company and also improve themselves. When employees feel better about themselves they are likely to feel better about their company. When employees feel good about their company, they are likely to contribute more to the success of their company.

I'm not suggesting that every employee will deliver excellent performance—there are too many contingencies that get in the way of that. However, I do believe that many employees can and will do a better job if they are expected, encouraged, and inspired to do so. Mentoring people is directly correlated to inspiring employees to improve their performance.

Research shows that mentored employees will be more responsive to management, helping to pull the team together, commit to the company and its mission, and transcending narrow personal interests. The resulting workforces are far more willing to collaborate and are better at identifying important challenges and opportunities.

One reason that mentored employees stand out is that they know how to enlist other employees' desire to share in accountability for the company's successes and failures.

The effective mentoring program must embrace an intellectually stimulating environment. The experience should be grounded in real-world practical experiences. The mentee should believe that working within this relationship provides a safe and comfortable place to express his or her real career aspirations. The program should offer an inspiring experience with intellectually honest dialogue regarding personal responsibility and accountability. The discussion should be enlightening and result in a strengthening linkage between the mentee's personal leadership and the organization's performance.

As a result of intense engagement, each of the mentoring sessions should be challenging and invigorating. The mentee should always view the mentoring sessions as a rewarding experience and one that continuously inspires him or her to value the pursuit of excellence and maximize personal achievement.

In today's globally competitive world, knowledge and its management are key indicator of long-term success. Corporations and individuals are seeking knowledge-intensive solutions to sustain their competitive advantage. Forward-looking corporations and high-aspiration individuals recognize the need for professional mentoring and personal leadership development to support their ambitions.

Businesses that consistently invest in their people develop sustainable, long-term, competitive advantages over those organizations that do not. The reward for those organizations that invest in mentoring is there for the taking. And it makes life in organizations more fun and more motivating for all involved.

Manager's Checklist for Chapter 14

☑ Managers must remain mindful that successful mentees may be envied.

☑ Managers should remember that mentoring is not a reward for hard work; it is a way to help talented employees excel, to the benefit of all.

☑ Make sure you establish an appropriate budget for your mentoring program.

☑ Minimize the bureaucracy when establishing formal mentoring programs.

☑ Develop clearly defined objectives for each participant in each mentoring relationship.

☑ Build a culture that supports mentoring.

Principles of Leadership for Mentors

Whether you are a mentor or a mentee looking for a mentor, there are certain traits of leadership that characterize those who make the best mentors. These are the traits that will most likely lead to personal and organizational success. XCEO has identified eleven principles of leadership that define these traits. We present these here to stimulate your thinking and reinforce their importance.

Principle One

Leaders have a passion for developing people. They are in constant pursuit of every employee's success. X-Leaders do not declare total victory until all the people around them have succeeded.

Principle Two

Leaders find imaginative ways to inspire people to transform themselves for the better. They motivate themselves and others to reach higher levels of performance by linking great ideas to exhilarating images of success.

Principle Three

Leaders cultivate creativity by looking at common things in uncommon ways. They expose old issues to new options and develop fresh approaches to long-standing problems.

Principle Four

Leaders are customer-centric; they realize that unless someone buys something from their company, everything they do is totally irrelevant.

Principle Five

Leaders are visionaries who anticipate the future and identify marketplace opportunities before they become trends. Leaders often know what customers will need before the customers do.

Principle Six

Leaders drive their companies with decisions grounded in facts. They insist on exchanging information with all employees and customers, and they seek opportunities to tell the truth.

Principle Seven

Leaders have confidence in the abilities of their people. Because leaders are willing to delegate broad responsibilities, they are vulnerable, and they know it.

Principle Eight

Leaders convert the energy generated by chaos into better decisions. To avoid precipitating premature closure on major issues, they sometimes conceal their own opinions until other people have had their say.

Principle Nine

Leaders believe that the company comes first, and they insist on teamwork. They do not tolerate divisional or functional departmental boundaries in the corporate culture.

Principle Ten

Leaders expect greatness. They are results-oriented, honest, and personally accountable.

Principle Eleven

Leaders are role models. They lead by example.

Index

About the Author

Dr. Curtis J. Crawford is president and CEO of XCEO, Inc. He is also the author of *Corporate Rise: The X Principles of Extreme Personal Leadership* and *Compliance & Conviction: The Evolution of Enlightened Corporate Governance.*

Dr. Crawford currently serves on the board of directors of E. I. du Pont de Nemours, ITT Corporation, and ON Semiconductor. He is also a trustee of DePaul University. He has served on the board of directors of Agilysys, Lyondell Petrochemical, and The Sisters of Mercy Health Corporation.

He has served as chairman of the board of ON Semiconductor; chairman, president, and CEO of Zilog; president, CEO, and director of Onix Microsystems, and chairman of the board of ISTAT. Dr. Crawford also serves as a special advisor to several startup companies.

He began his career as a systems engineer at IBM. Over 15 years, he held executive positions, including vice president of marketing. During a 10-year tenure, Dr. Crawford was group president of the Microelectronics Group and president of the Intellectual Property division of AT&T and Lucent Technologies.

Dr. Crawford earned a BA in Business Administration and Computer Sciences and an MA in Business from Governors State University. He earned an MBA from the Charles H. Kellstadt Graduate School of Business at DePaul University and a Ph.D. in Organization and Management from Capella University. In addition, Dr. Crawford has been awarded two honorary doctorate degrees, one from Governors State University and the other from DePaul University.